1991
Country Home
Collection

Country Home

Editor in Chief: Jean LemMon
Managing Editor: Ann Omvig Maine
Art Director: Peggy Fisher

Building Editor: Steve Cooper
Home Furnishings Editor: Candace Ord Manroe
Interior Design Editor: Joseph Boehm
Food and Garden Editor: Molly Culbertson
Antiques and Collectibles Editor: Linda Joan Smith
Features Editor: Beverly Hawkins
Assistant Art Director: Sue Mattes
Copy Chief: Dave Kurns
Copy Editors: Michelle Sillman, Greg Philby
Administrative Assistant: Becky A. Brame
Art Business Clerk: Jacalyn M. Mason

Contributing Editors
Barbara Cathcart, Joan Dektar, Eileen Alexandra Deymier,
Mary Didio, Estelle Bond Guralnick, Sharon Haven,
Helen Heitkamp, Cathy Howard, Merilyn Howard, Nancy Ingram,
Bonnie Maharam, Trish Maharam, Amy Muzzy Malin,
Mindy Pantiel, Ruth L. Reiter, Sharon Ross, Pat Schudy,
Mary Anne Thomson, Bonnie Warren

Publisher: Terry McIntyre
Senior Vice President/Publishing Director: Adolph Auerbacher
Vice President/Operations: Dean Pieters
Vice President/Editorial Director: Doris Eby
President/Magazine Group: James A. Autry

BETTER HOMES AND GARDENS® BOOKS
Editor: Gerald M. Knox
Art Director: Ernest Shelton
Managing Editor: David A. Kirchner

President, Book Group: Jeramy Landauer
Vice President, Retail Marketing: Jamie L. Martin
Vice President, Administrative Services: Rick Rundall

MEREDITH CORPORATION OFFICERS
Chairman of the Executive Committee: E.T. Meredith III
Chairman of the Board: Robert A. Burnett
President and Chief Executive Officer: Jack D. Rehm

1991 COUNTRY HOME® COLLECTION
Editor: Jean LemMon
Project Editor: Marsha Jahns
Graphic Designer: Mary Schlueter Bendgen
Electronic Text Processor: Paula Forest

Contents

A Midwest island retreat
that pays tribute to architect Frank Lloyd
Wright. A 155-year-old New England barn that
was razed and reconstructed. A log cabin
that serves as guest house and classroom. A
summer home overlooking the ocean that's
been shared by five generations of a
family. Each of these homes—and 14 others
featured on the pages of the *1991 Country
Home Collection*® celebrates American country
style: its comfort, its versatility, and its ties
to our history, heritage, ethnic roots, and
regionality. Besides these distinctive homes, showcased in *Country Home*® magazine during
1990, this third annual edition of the *Collection*
expands its focus to include a trio of beautiful
country gardens.

February

Country Home

Return to Clamshell Road

Style Is No Barrier

A Slice of Wright

Return To Clamshell Road

By Candace Ord Manroe. Produced by Bonnie Maharam

Now restored to its mid-1800s character, the Pritchard home recalls a colorful heritage of clamming on the New Jersey seashore.

Nearly every time she sifts through the loose soil in her garden, Pat Pritchard brushes across a bony contour that's ridged and rough to the hand. Hairy bristles are sprinkled across its back, but Pat doesn't flinch. The object is simply a refresher course in local history.

Pat's fingers have unearthed a clamshell, a telling vestige from the days when her Fair Haven, New Jersey, homesite was in the

Top: *Pat and Paul Pritchard spent 16 years restoring their late-Federal home, above.*
Left: *Discovered in the backyard, the mantel was returned to its den hearth.*

7

Return To Clamshell Road

thriving middle of a busy clamming industry; days when Pat's street—the town's first—bore the fittingly colorful name, Clamshell Road.

"No one can garden in this town without running across clamshells," says Pat. Just down the street from her home is the dock, "restored to its original condition," from which the clams were shipped on steamers to New York, she explains.

Fair Haven started in 1620 as part of Shrewsbury township, one of New Jersey's oldest. "But almost nothing from that period remains," says Pat.

Instead, the earliest extant architecture dates from the mid-19th century—the same period as the Pritchard home. The home not only is important as an example of that era's architecture but also as part of an even larger historical entity. Its address is on a street that is one of the few in New Jersey whose buildings appear as they did before the Civil War.

Top: According to custom, the first owners topped their mahogany baluster with a medallion when the mortgage was paid.
Above: Antique Chippendale chairs flank a circa-1790 Queen Anne tea table in the living room.
Right: An antiques dealer found the living room's 18th-century highboy in a Dairy Queen.

Return To Clamshell Road

The Pritchard home in particular is unchanged. Before Pat and her husband, Paul, bought the house, only one other family, the Hendricksons, had lived there. The last members of that family lived to be 100 and 104 years old.

"After that, the house remained empty for 10 years, then was sold at a sheriff's auction to pay off back taxes," says Pat.

The buyer never moved into the home but remodeled it to resell.

"He put in plumbing, heat, and electricity. The Hendricksons had never had those conveniences," Pat explains.

In addition, the second owner postponed major restoration work in favor of a superficial cover-up, which the Pritchards promptly set about to uncover.

"When the moving truck arrived at the house, my husband and son were already ripping out the paneling the previous owner

Left: *Wide-board floors and double-hung windows that dip into the wainscoting are part of the original dining room. A circa-1780 New England sawbuck table is surrounded by Windsor-style chairs—the home's only reproductions.* Above: *Blue paint flecks the 18th-century New England step-back cupboard.*

11

Return To Clamshell Road

had put in. That started the restoration that went on, in stages, for the next 16 years," says Pat.

Like most restorations, this one was not without its moments. For starters, there was the simple fact that the couple had three sons—two were small, and the oldest was in high school.

"After my husband and son were about five minutes into ripping off the paneling when we were moving in, one of our other sons fell out of an apple tree and broke his arm," recalls Pat.

And somewhere into the major house redo Paul went into business for himself, "which added to the tension," Pat says, and it required them to get some outside aid from local carpenters and craftsmen. Fortunately, the Pritchards were able to retain the same carpentry firm that had crafted the original woodwork for the Hendricksons.

"We were very lucky. Even though a new generation of owners had taken over, they had

Top: *The same type of brick pavers that appear on the kitchen floor graces patios and sidewalks for a smooth transition between inside and out.*
Above: *The kitchen cabinetry is made of 250-year-old pine.*
Right: *Countertops gain a country feel from the splattered appearance of a rare Bahia blue granite from Italy.*

Return To Clamshell Road

all of the old records from this house," says Pat.

After giving the living and dining rooms a cosmetic cleanup, the Pritchards put them to their original use. However, they adapted the kitchen into a small den and then created a new kitchen space from the original woodshed, gutting it to reveal old ceiling beams.

One of five tiny bedrooms was converted into a large bathroom, and an L-shape wing was added with a family/game room and two additional bedrooms and bathrooms. This new wing conforms to the original lines of the architecture, merely extending those lines farther out. Finally, the family added a sun porch, patio, and pool.

The additions lack the raw appearance of many new spaces, perhaps because of how they were sited. "Everywhere we put additions, there had originally been sheds. These had been removed when they were condemned by the city in the 1960s," explains Pat.

Left: *The couple's first antique, a small 18th-century worktable with red paint, appears with circa-1800 birdcage Windsor chairs in the sun porch.*
Above: *An 18th-century green roundabout chair and six-board blanket chest with remarkably preserved original painted decoration continue the room's lighthearted mood.*

Return To Clamshell Road

After taking such lengths to preserve the home's architectural integrity, the Pritchards naturally wanted to maintain similarly high standards in the home's interior design.

They've been antiques collectors since their marriage, when they lived in Marblehead, Massachusetts. Their furnishings are all New England pieces from the 18th and early 19th centuries. Creating charming spaces compatible with the home, then, wasn't really a matter of decorating. It was simply utilizing those vintage pieces lovingly assembled over the last 30 years.

Some formal pieces—a Queen Anne tea table and Chippendale chairs in the living room—furnish the home. But an abundance of warmth pervades through the simple lines of country Chippendale chairs, the weathered patina of chipped-paint cupboards and chests, and collections of pewter and other colonial accents.

The results of such careful readying: Old Clamshell Road never looked better. □

Right: In the original master bedroom, an early 1700s tavern table hugs the wall behind two wing chairs. The original wide-board pine floors complement a late-1700s chest. Above: A rare mid-1700s Connecticut folding or press bed appears in an upstairs bedroom. Top: This bath originally was a bedroom.

STYLE
Is No Barrier

By Steve Cooper. Produced by Estelle Bond Guralnick

When most of us build, we face inherent limitations, such as money, space, or family considerations. Those in wheelchairs face a common challenge: steering clear of an institutional-looking home.

Telltale signs are there: a few inches of extra floor space between cabinets; light switches installed a bit below standard height; bathroom vanities with a large well open beneath the countertop.

Alan Langer's Marblehead, Massachusetts, house has been designed to accommodate his motorized wheelchair. But unless one has a Holmesian penchant for snooping and deductive reasoning, there's no reason to notice.

"It's unfortunate, but a lot of people expect the handicapped to live in houses that look like hospital rooms. My home is an absolute haven for me. I don't want it to look like I live in an institution," Alan says in vibrant voice.

When Alan and his wife, Rachel, married in 1985, she already owned the converted 100-year-old barn/carriage house where the ceremony was held. After the newlyweds took up residence there, modifications had to be made for Alan's special needs. When the couple wed, he was still able to get around using a cane.

Left: *Alan and Rachel Langer and her daughter, Aryn, are joined by builder Ted Haggett. Ted sold the barn/carriage house to Rachel and later converted it to comfortable and expansive quarters for Rachel and Alan. Ted says, "A lot of builders don't want to tackle this kind of project because they know it's going to mean extra work and extra problems. They may worry that it won't be as profitable as conventional housing. But I found it to be a great project."*

Above: *Among the Langers'
favorite living room pieces are
the New Hampshire
barbershop sign and pole. Alan
says, "I wasn't too interested in
antiques before I met Rachel.
Now I've really got the bug."*
Left: *The Langers' Marblehead
home, not far from the town
square, was used as both a
carriage house and a barn
during its 100 years. A young
woman once stopped by to tell
Rachel, "I just want you to
know that I used to keep my
horse in your bedroom."*

STYLE
Is No Barrier

Now he is limited to his wheelchair and has only minimal use of his arms.

More than a decade ago Alan was diagnosed as having multiple sclerosis, a degenerative disease striking the nervous system. Though it has slowly taken away his mobility, it has done little to dampen his energetic enthusiasm for living. He continually amazes Rachel.

"The amount of energy he has is astonishing. He has good days and bad days just like everybody else. But he never gets angry about his disability. That's just life to him. Another challenge. Another opportunity," she says.

After their marriage, their home needed major modification. Rachel had been living only on the first floor. The second floor was little more than open rafters where the two large bedrooms would go. Also, Alan needed a chair lift to get him up and down. The couple and their

builder, Ted Haggett, from nearby Merrimac, plunged into the job.

"It rained sawdust on me for quite a while there," Alan says. Rachel remembers coming home each day at lunchtime to brush the rubble off her husband.

The greatest hurdle was shoring up the aging sides of the building, which bowed under the roof's weight. After the walls were pulled into alignment, they were stabilized with a 30-foot beam.

With the structure solidified, Ted turned his attention to the staircase. Since the lift required a straight run, switchback stairs had to go. The replacements were relocated to the end of the living room wall and spruced up by Ted with just the right touch—railings and post turnings from an old widow's walk. For 10 years, he had been saving the handsome pieces salvaged from a seaside dwelling.

"Over and over again, Ted did that

Left: *Though the kitchen floor is brick, Alan says it poses no problem for his wheelchair. "It's fairly smooth and easy to maneuver around on." Among the details that make the kitchen accessible to Alan are cabinets with slide-out shelves and pantry doors that fold back completely flat when open. That's an often-missed point, Alan says. Shelves must clear the doors so Alan can reach all essentials. "I'll never starve to death, that's for sure."*

Above: *Rachel brought to the marriage a collection of antiques and family furniture, including the dining room cabinet and side chairs. Alan's contributions were more modern, such this glass-top table.* Left: *Wooden kitchen utensils are only one of the couple's collections. A wall in their dining room is covered with wooden cutting boards and breadboards. They also have some old parlor games, including Around the World with the Amazing Nelly Bly. Alan says, "I just buy things that make me happy."*

STYLE
Is No Barrier

kind of thing for us. He'd come up with something he'd been saving and it would be perfect," Alan says.

Alan had a few tricks of his own, too: attractive brass ship fittings placed as grab bars in bathrooms; a shower large enough to accommodate a wheelchair; intercoms strategically placed for safety's sake; a pad-style thermostat control that Alan can punch with a mouth stick.

"You've got to make sure all the little things are done so you can live as comfortably as possible. Like the sink in the bathroom. It had to be raised enough so my knees wouldn't bang into it. Too many people put up with that kind of thing when they don't have to," says Alan, who serves on several governmental advisory commissions on handicapped issues.

Rachel adds, "People who have disabilities sometimes feel like they're Job. Like something's befallen them and they don't deserve good things. That's just not right."

To help correct this sadly self-limiting notion, the Langers formed a company, Independence Unlimited, which offers electric wheelchairs, stair lifts and a medical emergency alert system. They also consult on design for the handicapped.

Before MS forced him to work at home, Alan was a corporate management consultant. Now he's a consultant helping sensitize builders and disabled homeowners as to what's possible and practical.

"There's a tendency to think of the handicapped as a monolithic group. But we aren't all dealing with the same things. When it comes to a house, you have to ask questions like: Can you turn or pivot better to the right or to the left? That will determine things like where the grab bars will go. It can make all the difference in the world," he says.

There must also be an awareness that physical conditions may change. Alan himself has faced this problem. When he first installed the electric lift in the stairwell, he thought it would work out well. But soon he couldn't get on and off without help. An elevator would have been a wiser choice, he says.

But Alan won't let a drawback spoil his sense of independence.

"I've always wanted my house to be a place I could feel safe. My shelter against the rest of the world. Now, everything in my home makes me feel happy and secure. Why even the cat, Buffy, makes me happy. And that's saying something." □

Editor's note: *Because of the chair-lift problem, the Langers recently built another Marblehead house. Similar in style, the new home has an elevator.*

Above *and* left: *Before the conversion of the barn/carriage house began, the bedroom was little more than an open loft. Now it is a haven of rest. There are two 20×13-foot bedrooms upstairs. The master bath has Mexican floor tiles, brass grab bars, and a shower stall large enough to accommodate a wheelchair. The second bedroom is Aryn's, who is off at her first year of college. Alan says, "I credit Rachel for our home. She has a sixth sense for good taste."*

Left: *The stairwell behind the rocking horse is equipped with an electric lift and Alan has to keep a wheelchair on each floor. (The difficult transfer recently forced the Langers to build a new home where they installed an easy-to-operate elevator that Alan can control alone.) Of their barn/carriage house, Alan says, "If I was listing my preferences of all the places I've ever lived, this one would be right at the top. Before I ever met Rachel, I sketched the house I wanted to live in, and it looked just like this."*

A SLICE OF
WRIGHT

By Steve Cooper
Produced with Jean LemMon and Polly Minick

It's a lazy afternoon in the late 1940s, and a 12-year-old boy has his nose buried in a book about architect Frank Lloyd Wright. The boy, swept up in the grandeur of the designs and the designer, imagines himself as the next master to orchestrate symphonies of stone and steel.

But the boy never became an architect. Instead, Tom Monaghan made pizza. As founder and chairman of the board of Domino's Pizza, his building blocks have been pepperoni and mozzarella. However, he never forgot those afternoons transported by the heady, philosophical renderings.

"It was the pictures that caught my eye at first. Then I just read and read. Frank Lloyd Wright had this incredible talent, and he followed his own instincts. He was a free spirit, and his work didn't follow conventions. His creativity attracted me," says Tom.

Though it was a pan rather than a

Opposite: *In the Monaghans' Michigan vacation home, the bold verticals and horizontals of this Frank Lloyd Wright side chair and the framed fabric offer strong, appealing counterpoint to a rustic table by furniture maker Ken Heitz. The oak straight-back chair is from Wright's 1909 Robert Evans house in Longwood, Illinois. The fabric is from F. Schumacher & Company's Taliesin Line manufactured in 1955. Above: Tom and Marge Monaghan relax outside their retreat on tranquil Drummond Island in Lake Huron. Sailing, fishing, and seclusion are the main island attractions.*

pen for him, Tom's admiration for Wright's soaring spans and arresting ambitions was ever-present.

As a teenager, Tom got his first glimpse into a Wright home. Later, as a Marine stationed in Japan, he explored Wright's Imperial Hotel in Tokyo, although he couldn't afford a room. Years later, he took Marge, his wife, and their young daughters on the family's first vacation: a motor tour of Wright homes scattered around the Midwest.

"Walking around a Wright home has always been an emotional thing for me. They've become like old friends," he says.

Though his career wasn't drawn into architecture, Tom's pizza business has delivered a comfortable life. By the mid-1980s he could afford to indulge his Wright passion. He began hungrily collecting Wright-designed articles, but not merely to satisfy an appetite

Photographs: Jim Hedrich, Hedrich-Blessing; portrait and exterior house photograph, Jim Kelley.

for acquisition. Like Wright, Tom takes delight in enriching others.

"There's a tremendous satisfaction in seeing other people gaining the kind of appreciation for Frank Lloyd Wright that I have; to understand all his contributions," Tom says.

Toward that end, he founded the National Center for the Study of Frank Lloyd Wright at Domino's Ann Arbor, Michigan, headquarters. Open to the public is Tom's multimillion-dollar collection of Wright-designed objects, including chairs, tables, fabrics, tableware, art glass windows, and Wright's custom Cherokee-red 1940 Lincoln Continental.

"It would probably be better if all of his houses could be restored as they originally stood, so people could enjoy them as they were meant to be seen. Unfortunately, that's not always possible: It depends who owns them; what's happened to the furnishings; those kinds of things," he says.

So he collects to preserve. But there's something obviously missing from Tom's impressive museum list.

"I didn't have a Wright house. I've dreamt of living in one since I first saw his work in a library book," he says.

Though he scoured the country, the right Wright couldn't be found. So Tom did the next best thing: He commissioned his 1985 vacation home to be designed in Wright's style.

"I wanted something in the forest style that Wright did before World War I. It looks good there in the woods. It captures that sense of repose that nothing but a Wright seems to," Tom says.

The home settles into a hillside on

Opposite: *Patterns in the living room reflect Tom's interest in Native American culture.* Above right: *Warmth is added with a local-stone fireplace. The red-and-black plate is a Pat Charley original.* Right: *Shadows add still more lines to the house designed by a former Wright student, architect Bruce Johnson. Copper-pressing equipment was moved to the island to form the distinctive batten-pattern roofing.*

A SLICE OF WRIGHT

Drummond Island, Michigan, which borders Canada in Lake Huron. Tom and Marge try to get in a weekend of island life each month.

"I enjoy it there more than anywhere else I know of," says Tom, enthusiasm quickening his voice.

And why not? Drummond, a 20×14-mile freshwater island, offers postcard-perfect panoramas of lake and forest. It's the kind of place where a person can fish all day, not catch a thing, and still be as content as a salmon in cool water.

Though it is only about 100 yards from the Monaghan house to one of Drummond's bays, the lake cannot be seen through the thick growth of swaying pines. From water's edge, trees along the Canadian shoreline are just visible across the great blue lake.

With true Wrightian character, the house both imposes and poses. It captures terrain while blending into it. It feels at once heavy enough to have come from the earth yet light enough to rise above it. It's a comfortable, contradictory palette of ideas.

"I wanted it to reflect Wright's early work, to capture his spirit," Tom says.

The house echoes the side of Wright that preferred rural rhythms to city life. Always a country boy at heart, Wright envisioned the perfect city as a place where each home would occupy a richly planted acre of land. Like the Monaghan house, each would exhibit an organic architecture; that is, structures would nestle harmoniously into their environment.

With heavy, horizontal decks jutting from every side, Tom's house bears a resemblance to Fallingwater, Wright's

Opposite: *The glow of the sun descending 16 feet from a skylight brightens the compact kitchen. Perfect for vacations, everything is easily at hand in this small U-shape workplace. There's a forest view from the sink. The wake-up colors of fiestaware are a favorite of Tom's.* Left: *An informal snack for two is right at home in the eating nook opposite the kitchen or on the deck outside. Built-in seating is mounted beneath the windows.*

A SLICE OF WRIGHT

1936 plane-geometry gem levitating above a Pennsylvania brook.

Also like a true Wright, Tom's is a feast of primal elements: Its pine is from surrrounding forests; the rock was quarried locally; and a copper roof was burnished by rain and sun. These various textures blend with moody shadows and a sense of outback isolation.

Yet, the space never engender the felling they are unsophisticated or crude—just the opposite. Both the exterior and the Monoghan's room arrangements are on the Wright mark.

If the floor plan ha a first and most prominent use, it is as a stage for conversation, entertaining and relaxing.

The living room is a 32x21-foot expanse of Canadian pine. Guests may gather in the sunken seating area around a rock fireplace, lounge along 14 feet of built-in bank seating nestled against a wall of windows, or sample small talk around a table at the rear of the room.

Tom's interest in Native American culture is reflected in the chioce of fabrics for pillows and rugs. Living room, surfaces are softened by these linear, Southwest designs.

The room's ceiling is an unexpected treat as it hangs low enough to touch in one spot while soaring 20 feet in another.

The living room consumes most of the upper floor. THere iass a modest bedroom woth a fireplace. The kitchen and bath are smaller than modest. They are downright dinky. But that isn't a problem in a house intended primarily for vacations.

Bedrooms for each of the four Monoghan daughters take up the lower floor. Each rustic-bunkhouse-style room has its own bath.

Although the house fits into the style Tom dearly loves, he admits Wright's idiosyncrasies are not for everyone. Marge, for instance.

"Margies's never been too thrilled with Frank Lloyd Wright. I did get her to go to Fallingwater with me once, and she admitted she like it. But every time I reminded her she said that, she's quick to point out that she might like it, but she'd never live in it," says Tom, Margie's husband of 27 years.

Tom fells just as strongly. For him, Wright's designs are never wrong.

He says: "I tend to overlook his weak points. I know he went from wife to wife and had no discipline to his finances. But his talent was incredible.

"The beauty of Frank Lloyd Wright's houses was never one thing. It was the sum total. A Wright house is always a whole composition."

Above: *A second main-floor fireplace warms the Monoghan's bedroom. "Wright loved to fit in as many fireplaces as he could," Tom says. Unlike some of Wright homes, the bedroom is big enough for a bed, built-in desk, and closets. The esteemed architect wasn't convinced closets were a necessity.*

April

Country Home

Head of the Class
Where the Good Old Boys Gathered
High Pasture

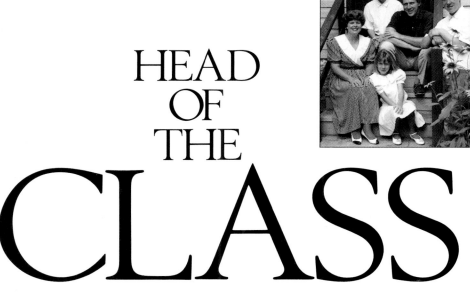

HEAD OF THE CLASS

The farmhouse of two Maryland teachers gets high marks for restored beauty

By Steve Cooper. Produced by Eileen Deymier

Far left: *The front porch of the Swam farm, furnished simply with primitive rockers, offers the perfect spot to relax on a hot summer day. One gets a clear view of the handsome stone-end barn, which may be slightly older than the house.*
Top: *Norma Jean and Carroll Swam with their daughter, Carrie, and sons, Chris, left, and Jason.*
Left: *The red-brick farmhouse appears much as it did when it was built about 1854. The small building at left was once a summer kitchen.*

Living at Red Brick Farm in Millers, Maryland, has been an education for Carroll and Norma Jean Swam.

The two school teachers were engaged when they bought their 1850s brick farmhouse, barn, and 25-acre spread in 1969. The structures were sturdy, but living spaces were in shambles. A thousand baby chicks had once roosted in the sitting room.

Rubberized floor tiles covered original wood floors. Piles of burned trash littered the grounds.

"I remember when Norma Jean's parents first came up here. I think they were ready to talk her out of marrying me. Even my friends thought I was a bit crazy," Carroll says.

But they persevered.

"We had the basics—a heating plant and plumbing in the house.

Those things kept it manageable, and we could do the house a little bit at a time as time and money allowed," he says.

The result is a serene, rural oasis. Though surrounded by an invading, homogenizing suburbia, Red Brick Farm quenches the thirst for a kind of peace earned only through hard work.

The Swams have made the 19th-century farm

33

HEAD OF THE CLASS

their own by restoring the beauty of the grounds, refurbishing the stonework on the barn, and building a kitchen/eating area addition.

"Before Carroll ever bought the place, we decided it was just about the biggest project we could handle. It stretched us to our limit at times, but the end result has been worth it," Norma Jean says.

The farm takes its name from the red bricks made on the property and employed in the architecture. Both the house and barn were built around the same time by farmer Jacob Frederick Shaffer, who established his estate with 300 acres.

The Swams are fortunate to have a black-and-white photograph of the farm as it was about 1920. The picture, which was given to them by a former resident of the house, serves as a valuable blueprint guiding them in their renovation.

"When we wanted to rebuild the small porch which had fallen off years before we bought the farm, we debated whether to put a double porch on. But we decided not to because that was not the way the house had been originally," Norma Jean says.

As teachers, they brought advantages and disadvantages to their renovation. On the positive side, they had summer months free. Public school salaries, however, make

Left: *The space occupied by this cozy sitting room was part of the kitchen for several years. In 1984, the Swams moved the kitchen into an addition. Norma Jean says, "When we added the new kitchen, we knew we wanted another room off the kitchen to serve coffee after dinner and such. We really do use the room a lot. It's a nice place to just sit and read." Her collection of Adams china, made between 1790 and 1820, is displayed on the cupboard.*

Top: *Carroll and Norma Jean pooled their Christmas money one year to buy the imposing cherry corner cabinet. The table flips open to double size. Trim colors throughout the house are the same as those found originally at Red Brick Farm.*

Above: *The simple desk in the entry hallway was purchased in Connecticut. Hanging above it is a picture of the farm as it appeared about 1920. The photo has guided the home's renovation.*

HEAD OF THE CLASS

budget watching a requirement.

They started with the main living space on the first floor. For nearly two years, their kitchen and one of four upstairs bedrooms were their primary living spaces. The rest of the farmhouse was under a state of siege.

"We began gradually going room by room, peeling back wallpaper and removing all the things that weren't appropriate to the house. All the woodwork, doors, mantels, and about eighty percent of the hardware is original," says Carroll.

It was a dirty, tough job that was often deceptive; such as the time Carroll and a friend started ripping out fireplace brick to uncover an earlier fireplace. Carroll told Norma Jean it would be a snap. But by the time he was done, he had removed two pickup-truck loads.

Carroll, who grew up in older houses, had a general idea about restoration work before he bought the home. But he learned mostly by doing.

"I certainly knew what could go wrong with an old house, and I had a little bit of experience with construction. But I wouldn't say I was an expert or anything," he says.

The couple also had much to learn about decorating. In the early 1970s, much less information was available about restoration decor,

Left: *A growing family and a large microwave oven finally became too much for the farmhouse's small, original kitchen. So this spacious addition was built. The inch-thick cherry cabinets were built by Carroll's cousin, Lewin Masemore. Norma Jean says the center island is the kitchen's best feature. "When we have company, I can be preparing the meal while guests sit around the table. No one is in the way, and yet I'm not cut off from my guests."*

Top: *This small eating area in the kitchen addition is graced by one of the Swams' favorite furniture pieces, a Pennsylvania step-back cupboard. Though it was love at first sight, the couple had to buy it on a layaway plan. Perseverance pays.*

Above: *Norma Jean is particularly fond of this Amish clothing. As a teacher, she uses it to give schoolchildren a better grasp of Amish self-sufficiency.*

37

HEAD OF THE CLASS

but they ferreted out information and began collecting room ideas.

"Over the years we traveled and went to museums and living history farms. . . . We kept our eyes open and we developed friendships with people who were doing the same kinds of things. We were able to help each other," says Norma Jean.

One recommendation they'd make for budget-conscious couples is to forgo Christmas gift exchanges. Instead, pool the money and invest in something extravagant for the house.

Their major project came in 1984, when they built an 18×20-foot kitchen addition to replace the cramped original facilities. The old kitchen's breaking point was reached when Carroll brought home a too-big microwave oven.

"There just wasn't anyplace for it, so we had to build a new kitchen. All I wanted was a microwave, but I got a kitchen," Norma Jean says.

To match the aging grace of the rest of the house, the Swams used recycled materials wherever possible. Salvaged doors were utilized. Flooring came from a nearby lodge hall facing demolition. When all was done, the Swams felt the addition looked even older than their farmhouse.

"We have three kids and we can't live in a museum.

Left: *When the Swams bought the farm, this master bedroom had a conventional flat ceiling. It was so badly deteriorated, they tore it out. With the ceiling now rising to the peak of the roofline, it was possible to create the small loft. The couple bought the bed in an antiques shop simply because they liked it. Not until they were setting it up at home did they discover a nameplate stating it had been built in Pennsylvania during the same era as their farm.*

Top: *Norma Jean thinks of this low-roofed hideaway room off the master bedroom as something out of* Alice in Wonderland. *A staircase immediately inside the room provides access to the kitchen.*

Above: *When Carroll bought a pile of doors at an auction for $1, this grain-painted door and three like it were among the booty. This door separates the kitchen from a small sitting area. Carroll believes it was made in the 1820s.*

HEAD OF THE CLASS

But we tried to make the addition as compatible as possible with the old house," Norma Jean says.

With the success of Red Brick Farm under their belts, Carroll and sons have ventured into projects beyond their own property. In recent years, they have started a renovation business specializing in moving old log structures.

As an amateur becoming an expert, Carroll has tips for others with similar ambitions. Go slow, he says. Haste will ruin the best intentions.

"Let the house speak to you. You don't want to change too much

unnecessarily. Also, make sure what you change is reversible," he recommends.

As you gradually make changes, do what work you can yourself. Save money and gain an understanding of houses.

Norma Jean also stresses the need for research. Tour other houses in the area and museums. Track down old pictures of your house and the era in which it was built. Educate yourself.

"Finally, you've got to be able to live with a certain amount of clutter, plaster, and so on. Sometimes when you're really tired of working on

the house, you have to take a break and wait. Enjoy what you've accomplished," she says.

That's solid advice from two teachers who score straight A's with their Red Brick Farm. □

Top: *Carroll bought this log structure, which is used as a garden shed by Norma Jean, for $1 at an auction. He and one of his sons took the building apart, numbered the pieces, and reassembled it.* Above: *With much of the interior work complete, Norma Jean had time last summer to start her herb garden. She uses some of her produce for cooking and dries the rest.*

WHERE THE GOOD OLD BOYS
GATHERED

Take a nostalgic look at the legacy of Legler Benbough, lifelong bachelor, antiques collector, and party giver.

By Mike McLuen. Produced by Sharon Haven

Above: *This veranda adds to the shady, leisurely ambience of the ranch house, tucked amid grassy meadows and eucalypti 20 miles north of San Diego (as the seagull flies).* Top: *The yoke mounted above the entryway served as a symbol of the Benbough ranch. It was used on his personal stationery and maps he sent to friends who hadn't yet discovered his hideaway.*

Photographs: Tommy Miyaski. Produced with Ann Omvig Manternach

Good Old Boys

Back in the late '30s, bachelor Legler Benbough began a love affair—with a 20-acre ranch he bought on a whim. Legler, son of San Diego Mayor Percy Benbough, was occupying comfortable quarters—the city's grand Hotel del Coronado—when he heard about the ranch. His passion for horses lured him to the property with its riding trails weaving among secluded wooded acres. It was ideal.

Part of the ranch had been planted in avocados and apples, but it was the towering eucalyptus trees that added an elegance and irresistible charm for Legler. He was captivated by the land; both its beauty and potential.

Although the ranch had a house, it was small and had never been occupied. There was not even a road into the place. But Legler soon remedied that by building a road, stables, and a caretakers' cottage. He moved his horses in and began to spend a great deal of time there himself. With no wife to act as hostess, he found the ranch was a perfect place to gather and entertain his energetic circle of friends, but the house wasn't quite big enough for socializing the way he wanted.

"In those days I did a lot of entertaining," says Legler. "The place had many good riding trails and lots of pheasant. Everyone would pitch in, so it was easy to put a barbecue together. We also had large catered parties with orchestras.

❖ ❖ ❖

Left: *Two wing chairs brace for a cozy chat in front of an open fireplace in the "new" living room. There are 10,000 square feet in the meandering home, including two kitchens, two dining rooms, five bedrooms, each with a bath, seven living rooms, and 11 fireplaces.*
Top: *Legler selected inviting spots for games and decorated them with comfortable leather and wood chairs.*
Above: *Note the unusual windbreak on the right side of this historic desk.*

GOOD OLD BOYS

We grew our own berries and corn, which we picked fresh and served with barbecued steaks."

Over the years Legler added on to the house. Rooms were sometimes planned to display an antique he had purchased on one of his European expeditions or a local jaunt. The original ranch house had modern furnishings, and two grand pianos graced the living room back in those days. But Legler found that most of his friends were attracted to the cozy pine den, where he had stuck some old lamps, a few antiques, and a few pieces of Early American furniture. After dinner his friends would gather there for brandy or coffee and listen to his Victrola.

"I soon found that all my guests headed for that room upon arrival," he says, "so I figured if they liked it that much, I'd change the rest of the house." That's when Legler began his interest in antiques.

"I read books on antiques and traveled a lot, " says Legler. "I did a lot of buying in Italy for a while, but the customs process was so complicated that it became easier to buy here."

World War II interrupted Legler's antiques pursuit. He enlisted in the Navy.

During his days in the service, he loaned his ranch out to people for weeks or months, until they could find their own housing.

After the war, Legler stepped up his ranch-improvement efforts, adding rooms, antiques, outdoor patio areas and verandas, a pool,

❖ ❖ ❖

Right: *Legler designed his new dining room around accumulated antiques such as the Dutch bed he made into the fireplace seen here. It was the perfect room to show off his pewter.*
Above: *The kitchen in the new addition was designed for guests, who pitched in to clean and cook corn in the spacious country kitchen. Both the new kitchen and the new dining room feature an unusual straw ceiling treatment Legler found in France.*

GOOD OLD BOYS

 badminton courts, landscaping touches, and a two-story addition. It featured a new kitchen, dining room, living room, and master suite.

"Whenever I'd get bored, I'd add a room," he says. The two-story addition lent a leisurely, sprawling atmosphere to the home.

What looks like a modest, albeit meandering home from the outside is actually a maze of levels of living spaces, one flowing into another. New discoveries seem to await at every turn: rare Indian artifacts, antique clocks, and painted trunks. Brick floors, braided rugs, and beamed ceilings add coziness that belies the home's size. (There are five bedrooms, two kitchens, several living rooms, and 11 fireplaces.)

One bedroom overlooks the largest living room through a shuttered opening. During the ranch's heyday, Legler cleared the bedroom for an orchestra and used the living room as a dance hall. He frequently loaned out his ranch for charitable events.

Though Legler thrived on surrounding himself with friends, occasionally he felt a need for solitude. Today, a favorite recollection is dining alone in the evenings beside an outdoor fireplace, with a roaring fire and candlelight his only companions.

After 48 years, Legler turned the ranch over to a foundation that eventually sold it complete with contents. He says, "It was fun putting all these things together. I had forty-eight years of enjoyment from the ranch, now it's someone else's turn." □

✦ ✦ ✦

Left: *Legler searched a long time for the mahogany bed that he refinished for his bedroom. Part of the pine-paneled bedroom was built onto the original ranch house, giving the retreat a spacious masculine touch. Legler planned to occupy the master suite in the new addition, but after one night, he moved back here.*
Above: *Legler went to great lengths and expense to have his copper tub refitted to the plumbing. "No one ever used it," Legler says, "but it looks great."*

HIGH
Pasture

As colorful as its name, this stately home on the rugged Maine shore is synonymous with summer for the Earle family—and has been ever since it was built in 1907.

By Candace Ord Manroe
Produced with Joseph Boehm

At the turn of the century, summer meant more than a change of season for families along the East Coast. It was the time for lightening up and getting away. City homes were locked and left by folks eager to taste the freedom—and fun—awaiting them at their special summer escape.

For many of these New Yorkers, Philadelphians, and Bostonians, Maine was the preferred destination. With its spectacular coastline and just enough suggestion of hinterlands to feel liberatingly different, the

state soon was smattered with colonies of summer folks.

One such pocket was Ogunquit. With its rocky cliffs, rare sandy beaches, and close proximity (about 80 miles) to Boston, it offered all the features of a prime escape.

It was here that Philadelphians James M. and Alice P. Earle decided to build High Pasture, their homage to warmer weather. In a clearing surrounded by meadows and woods, and flanked to the rear by the sea, they built a clapboard home of sound proportions and classic, if simple, architecture. A place that the family could enjoy not for just a few

Opposite, top: *Third, fourth, and fifth generations of Earles rest on the property's original stone seat overlooking the cliffs: Owner Frances Earle with daughters Elinor Stearns, left, and Patty Ouimet and her daughter, Maeghan.*
Opposite, left: *Not long after High Pasture was built, the Earle sisters shaded themselves from summer sun on a stone bench still used today.*
Above: *High pasture looks much as it did more than 80 years ago, when first built for the Earle family.*
Left: *The classic lines of a Palladian window are softened by new fabrics on the window seat visible from the front door.*

Photographs: William Stites. Interior design: Joseph Boehm.

Above: *Comfortable old overstuffed sofas and chairs in the living room were updated last year with pale chintz slipcovers that denote the sunny season.*
Right: *A living room window seat, freshly festooned with new pillows, underscores the idea of a casual, meant-to-be-lived-in summer home.*
Opposite: *Nearly all of the furniture is original to the home, including the dining room's turn-of-the-century mahogany claw-foot table and rush-seat chairs. A lighter look was achieved with ruffled chintz cushions and a woven Irish rug.*
Opposite, far right: *Since 1907, the Earles have appreciated the Atlantic's majesty.*

summers but nearly an entire century—and with the promise of still more years to come.

"Growing up, High Pasture always was a part of my life," says a fourth-generation Earle, Elinor Stearns. "Our family spent every summer here, as did my father when he was a boy. There was something very special about being in what was originally our great-grandmother's house, still surrounded by her furnishings, her gardens, with so little changed over the years. Because of this continuity, family stories really came to life. More than anywhere, this meant home."

That sense of a second home as a comfortable haven was just what Alice Earle had in mind when she retained architect Horace Wells Sellors to design High Pasture.

In the true spirit of a summer place, he emphasized the outdoors, capturing views and breezes with expanses of windows and a large screened gallery. Verandas and balconies meander along the facade, blurring the boundary between untamed nature and tamed interior.

Not that nature was left entirely wild. The pounding surf at the base of 30-foot cliffs was countered, nearer the house, with graceful gardens

HIGH PASTURE

by Frederick Olmsted, who also designed Central Park. Today, many of Olmsted's old-fashioned roses still grow along garden trellises. Daylilies, astilbes, and peonies—all included in his plans, which now belong to the Smithsonian Institution—once again grace the garden, thanks to the efforts of the third-generation owner, Frances Earle (Elinor's mother).

Just as the home was built with a sensitivity to site, taking advantage of sea breezes, hazy vistas, and sweet garden scents, it also was designed to efficiently serve its summer residents in another regard. Almost ahead of its time, High Pasture was an early

prototype of the low-maintenance house.

Built-ins that were intrinsically attractive as architecture served an important function by reducing the need for furnishings. Built-in cabinets sufficed in lieu of china cupboards and sideboards in the dining room, while window seats in the living room, back gallery, and stairway landing eliminated the need for freestanding chairs—and still do.

Built-ins spared the Earles the difficulty of transporting furniture to Maine. Those furnishings that were brought to High Pasture were, for the most part, sturdy and casual—

nothing that would devastate the family too much, if broken en route.

Amazingly, those same furnishings still fill the home as the primary pieces today, creating a sense of time warp rare outside a museum.

"Nearly everything is the same," says Frances Earle.

"All of the iron beds, the hooked rugs [more venerated today than when new], the garden furniture—these are original to the home. Most of these furnishings would not have been appropriate in the [Earles'] Philadelphia house, but they were ideal for High Pasture," she says.

With so much tangible evidence of

Opposite: *Fragrant gardens have been an emphasis of High Pasture since the original grounds were planned by landscape architect Frederick Olmsted, who designed Central Park.*
Above: *The back porch is one of the few areas to have undergone any notable change since High Pasture was built: Its original copper-screened windows were replaced with flat panes. Last year's cosmetic update of the home produced a casual beach-house look with pale blue and white-striped cotton fabric on sofa and window seats.*
Left: *With its view of ocean and meadow, the porch is a favorite gathering spot.*

Above, right: *An upstairs guest room was swathed in pink-striped paper with coordinating bedding and upholstery fabrics, making it one of the cheeriest spaces at High Pasture. The bed and bureau are original to the home; the wicker is new.*
Opposite: *Mrs. Earle's bedroom received its fresh face entirely through cosmetics: The wall covering is new, but all furnishings are original. The room's lace-paneled French doors open onto a balcony that overlooks the sea, perpetuating the sense of romance that has characterized the home since the first Earle sisters made their annual trek from Philadelphia.*

the past permeating nearly every nook and cranny, High Pasture is a place for remembering; for reflecting on the lives and times of those now gone, to whom it once was home.

The first mistress of High Pasture was responsible for the family's legacy of summering in Maine (the home's blueprints name Alice Earle, not her husband, as the client), yet she wasn't able to enjoy the place for long. The house was completed in February 1907, just eight years before her death.

Her three daughters, Elinor, Mary, and Doris, continued the tradition of summering there, and it is these

women—the "aunts"—whom today's
family members recall most vividly.

And where memory fails, family
photo albums fill in.

Wonderfully preserved
photographs show the Earle aunts as
young women on leisurely strolls
along the seashore, dressed in high-
collared splendor and carrying
parasols to shade unflattering light.
Walks to the apple orchard and cider
press, horse-drawn buggy rides, and
quiet times alone on a cool stone
ledge with nothing but the sea and
the family dog are all captured on
film for current generations to
appreciate.

HIGH PASTURE

Some of the old photos are especially romantic, lending credence to certain family legends. (One tale has an Earle aunt courted at High Pasture by an Austrian count. When her family broke off the romance, the young woman allegedly took to her bed with depression symptoms that plagued her for the rest of her life.)

Richard Earle, son of "Aunt" Elinor, purchased the Maine house in 1956. He had spent every summer of his youth at High Pasture and convinced his wife, Frances, to live with him there year-round for three years, until his death in 1977.

Since then, Frances, a native Texan who maintains a year-round residence there in her hometown of Waco, has reinstituted the summer tradition in Maine. Joining her are her children and grandchildren, fourth- and fifth-generation Earles.

Except for differences in dress and hairstyles, not much obvious change has transpired with the passing of the years at High Pasture. The family still takes pride in its well-tended gardens. Favorite pastimes remain simple: excursions with a dog down shady woodland paths, or restful hours on the porch, watching the fog burn off over the sea.

Throughout the century, then, High Pasture has honored its original focus, celebrating summer more than ceremony.

If anything, the current generations have sharpened that focus. The home is more livable: Servants no longer tend the dinner table; the original furnishings, already casual, become more so in simple slipcovers; a carefree, bleached palette replaces the earlier, darker color scheme.

The result is that High Pasture meets the new needs of an old family happily, with no generation gap; Alice Earle's dream lives on. □

Opposite: *High Pasture is important for two major reasons: One, the continuity of its one-family owners, and, two, the continuity of its physical appearance for nearly a century.*
Above: *Originally covering more grounds, High Pasture now spans only 14 acres. But the most important areas, such as this intimate garden, are little changed.*
Left: *New wicker patio furniture on the stone terrace that flanks the front of the home provides a comfortable vantage point. The distinctive ledge was built from local cobblestones. Similar raised-mortar treatments are found on the home's stone window seats and benches.*

GARDENS OF THE

Senses

Herbalist Darlene Rook nurtures carefully re-created colonial-style gardens under the hot Oklahoma sun.

By Molly Culbertson
Produced by Nancy Ingram

In a small town near Oklahoma City, a living potpourri flourishes in colonial-style herb gardens. That these gardens thrive so well in this hot, dry climate is in itself surprising, but there's more: The period gardens stand behind a 1950s ranch house, whose ordinary exterior hides interiors that have been stripped of nearly all signs of modernism. This is the

home of gardener Darlene Rook and her husband, Charles, a couple who have devoted years to the study and the collection of Early American antiques.

About a decade ago, Darlene decided to put in the herb beds. She had not gardened before, but re-creating old-fashioned gardens seemed an appropriate extension of her passion for the past—a hunger that never was sated by her many collectibles. "Herbs are ageless," Darlene says. "If they could talk, oh, the

Above: *Darlene Rook sits at her 18th-century trestle table weaving wreaths of dried thyme, silver-king artemisia, and sage.*

Left: *To disguise the newness of their 1950s home, Darlene and Charles added architectural details, paints, and antique furnishings typical of 18th-century New England. The beams here in the keeping room are 100 years old; floors throughout are wide pine planks.*

Photographs: Gene Johnson

Left: *Pink and yellow yarrow borders a row of artemisia. Yarrow is also known as woundwort: Legend has it that Achilles used it to heal his soldiers' wounds during the Trojan War. The common name for artemisia is wormwood. This bitter herb was used centuries ago to cure indigestion and restore appetites. Today it's used in perfumes, beer, and vermouth.*

GARDENS OF THE
Senses

Top: *The culinary garden begins just outside the kitchen door. Borage, shown here, has bright blue flowers that Darlene uses in salads, desserts, and drinks.*

Above: *Though Charles gives the credit for the herb gardens to Darlene, he laid the railroad ties and brick walks and hauled in the topsoil. Darlene cares for the herbs, she says, but Charles does any heavy maintenance work.*

Right: *In the kitchen, Darlene's handmade dough ornaments and dried herbs adorn an Early American tavern table.*

tales they would tell. Their history and legends are fascinating."

Darlene began not in her backyard but in libraries, where she dug through old herbals and gardening manuals. "Our founding fathers counted herbs among the essentials of life," she says. "When they came to the New World, herb seeds were among their meager possessions; planting herbs was one of the first things they did."

Settlers had their favorites, among them basil, burnet, dill, fennel, marjoram, parsley, rosemary, savory, and thyme. Darlene studied the many uses of these herbs—for beverages, dyes, medicines, restoratives, and even pesticides.

A year after she'd begun her research, Darlene and Charles began digging up their backyard. They added topsoil, sand, peat moss, compost, fertilizer, and perlite to make the soil lighter, richer, and more porous—more like the soil the settlers found as they

developed the colonies.

Charles laid railroad ties and brick foot paths to border and divide two raised herb beds, one planned as a fragrance garden and the other as a kitchen garden. An 18-foot square, the fragrance garden is the larger of the two, the focal point of the backyard. The kitchen garden, just outside the back door, is a 9-foot square of culinary herbs.

Darlene didn't fill the beds the first season. "Start out easy with just a few herbs," she says. "Learn all you can about them. Then the pleasure they give will increase."

In the fragrance garden, Darlene planted yarrow, baby's-breath, lavender, and scented geraniums. "I love looking around at the soft grays, lavenders, and pinks—thinking to myself that women like me were doing this very same thing hundreds of years ago."

Darlene displays her garden's harvest throughout the house, where rooms are airy and open, painted in colonial colors,

Left: *Blue salvia grows around a stone bird, one of several antique statuaries adorning the herb beds. Blue salvia is one of the sages. In medieval times, it was believed that sage gave wisdom and improved the memory. It is said that when everything in a gardener's life is going well, the sage will flourish. But when things are bad, the herb's foliage will begin to droop.*

☙

GARDENS OF THE
Senses

floored with wide pine planks, and filled with 18th-century New England furnishings.

The delicate fragrance of herbs hangs over everything. Old wood bowls on the pine trestle table are filled with her potpourris. Herbs hang from the ceiling in bunches to dry. Wreaths line walls next to shelves full of reference books and herbals.

Basil, fennel, sage, chives, rosemary, thyme, mint, and savory are among Darlene's most prized culinary herbs. From the fragrance garden, she treasures rose geranium, the fragrant blooms of lavender, and the feathery grays of silverking artemisia and lamb's-ears for potpourris and wreaths.

"Herbs are so easy to grow, so undemanding and forgiving," Darlene says. "What I love are the unexpected pleasures of just being in the garden, working and brushing up against lemon thyme or a scented geranium. They send out the sweetest fragrance. I love to take time to discover the character of the garden and respond to its peacefulness." □

Top: *An old stone turtle seems to crawl—slowly—along the rail in front of flourishing thyme, yellow and pink yarrow, and silvery lavender.*

Above: *Darlene snips pink and yellow yarrow to take inside and hang to dry. The blooms will retain some of their color as they dry, making them valuable additions to arrangements.*

Right: *Charles' brick paths border and divide the garden beds. Darlene loves to wander here, brushing against the herbs to release their fragrances.*

June

Country Home®

The Compleat
Homemaker

Gabler's Farm

Penchant for
Permanence

In the Shadow
of the City

This Massachusetts home overflows with original handiwork. From stacked-stone walls to handcrafted furniture to freshly brewed soap, Rachel van Leer does it all.

The *Compleat* HOMEMAKER

By Steve Cooper. Produced by Estelle Bond Guralnick

Though Rachel van Leer might be called a home-maker, artist may be a more apt description. She's the Picasso of her palace. A Renoir with rock walls. A Gauguin in her garden. A Degas who makes both dinner and the dinner table.

Her daughter, Sarah, insists, "I tell her to tell people she's an artist, not a housewife, because she makes an art of everything she does at home."

But Rachel is not one to boast.

"Well, everything I do is functional and practical. Perhaps we could call [what I do] functional art," she says.

With her family's 10-acre Lincoln, Massachusetts, farm as her canvas, Rachel immerses herself in such diverse mediums as wood, stone, vegetable, reed, paint, and wool.

While others may seek to have it all, Rachel

Opposite: *Rachel van Leer's herb garden follows a colonial-era design. "I took herb classes and really learned my herbs, which I use now for vinegars, cooking, wreaths, and pressed flowers on writing cards," she says.* Above: *The front of the Van Leer home is graced with bricks laid by Rachel.* Left: *Karl and Rachel van Leer lean on split-rail fence they built.*

Above: *The library's Williamsburg-blue paneling was painted to match 14th-century Dutch tiles that came from Karl's grandfather's house in Amsterdam.*

Left: *The Van Leers enjoy pursuing pleasures at auctions. Among their finds are the painting above the living room fireplace, the antique Afghanistan rug, and the Queen Anne tea table in front of the sofa. Rachel gave the old ladder-back armchair a new splint seat. Near the windows is a piano, where Rachel applies skills from 10 years of lessons.*

Above left: *Rachel utilizes the bright sun of a living room bay window for her plants. "I don't see how you can ever have too many flowers," she says.*
Above right: *The star pattern came from a quilt book.*

wants to make it all. Her projects have been as diverse as designing her home and whipping up her favorite pizza. She has hooked rugs, made patchwork quilts, worked in bronze stenciling, built stone walls, canned, and crafted.

"I was always interested in the domestic arts. My grandmother taught me to knit and sew and I made my own clothes in high school. I could always use a needle. Some women find a needle very clumsy, but I didn't," she said.

She learned a secret for success when she was 10 and fell in love with painted trays. She thought they were the most beautiful objects in the world, but how could she get one? Make it herself.

"I bought a book and paints, and did it on my own," she says.

It's a formula she continued to follow. Get advice from experts, then do it yourself. She's found the best sources for information and instruction are courses through local adult education programs, community colleges, and museums.

"I'm always taking classes. Learning new things. It's my plan to take a minimum of two a year. But I've had years when I've taken ten," she says.

She took her first in the early 1950s, soon after her marriage to Karl van Leer, her high school sweetheart. He was stationed with the military in Alaska, and she discovered instruction in leatherwork was a sure cure for boredom.

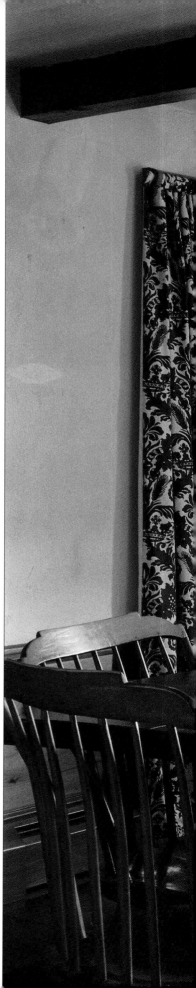

Above: *The blanket chest in the dining room was made in about 1700 and is still coated with its original buttermilk stain. To gain more display space for her metal wares, Rachel built the hanging cupboard and finished it with a matching stain.*

Right: *Rachel wanted just the right table and corner cupboard for her dining room, so she made them. She acquired woodworking skills at night courses at a regional high school, where she found other women taking classes, too. The table is a faithful copy of an elegant piece displayed at the Metropolitan Museum of Art in New York. She bought the chairs and antique bokhara rug at an auction.*

"As long as I've known Rachel, she's been busy doing something. It's in her genes. Her father was a farmer who went about his business sixteen hours a day and was the hardest-working man I've ever seen. She's just like him, and she enjoys every minute of it," says Karl, sales manager for Acorn Structures in Acton, Massachusetts.

When the Van Leers settled in Lincoln in 1958, Rachel's father gave them the land where they established their small farm. Though they live only 12 miles from downtown Boston, she says there is a Vermont ambience to the area's richly wooded hills and lush meadows.

Impressed by a gambrel-style home erected in Lincoln in the 1940s, Rachel designed her family's two-story, three-bedroom home to match its farmhouse look. With an eye toward their meager finances, the couple recycled some old barn lumber to build their house. As the family grew to include two sons and a daughter, the house also expanded with an addition enclosing a library, a master bedroom, and fireplaces.

Rachel's intent was to furnish her home with antiques. But the family budget couldn't stretch as

The Compleat HOMEMAKER

Above right: *For the kitchen eating area, Rachel built this 45-inch-round table by copying a smaller table.*
Above left: *The heart-shaped rug is Rachel's design. She braided it for a red-and-black upstairs bathroom.*

❖

far as her ambitions. So, she became a student again.

"In part, I was motivated by a desire to show my children they can do anything they want. They just need to apply themselves. It also may be that I'm some kind of a frustrated inventor. I like to figure things out. I see a basket and I want to know how it's made," she explains.

Among the most challenging and useful courses she has taken was woodworking. It is a skill she has applied to furniture, fences, and small handicrafts.

"I'm really glad I took it. But I like to do most of my woodwork at home with hand tools now. I've gotten rather skittish around big power tools. I began to catch on to the fact that there might be an issue here when I noticed how many of my instructors were missing a finger here or there," she says.

As a night-class veteran, Rachel has found the key to a good class is a good instructor. As she was learning the basics, she gained what she needed through public schools. But as she matured in her talents, she focused more on instruction offered

Above: *The sink counter in Rachel's kitchen comes alive with herbs from her garden. Lincoln blacksmith Ted Tucker made the wall bracket.*
Opposite: *This fireplace, tucked into a corner of the kitchen, gets the most use of the home's four fireplaces. Though rich in appearance, the panels are an inexpensive pine painted with a colonial red paint. The candle box was one of the first projects Rachel tackled using a handsaw.*

Left: *In her daughter's bedroom, Rachel keeps a Bates spread, a lap quilt, and pillows she crafted. On the antique dower chest at the foot of the bed is a cow weather vane from Rachel's father's barn.*
Above: *She also made these appliqué squares, which can be used for pillow covers or pieced together for a quilt.*

through museums. She now takes most of her classes through the DeCordova Museum in Lincoln.

"You have to approach craft instruction much the same way you approach any art instruction: Look for those teachers who know a great deal more than you do and know how to communicate. Get all you can from them and then move on to another teacher," she says.

Another of Rachel's secrets is her tenacity. She cannot be dissuaded from any undertaking.

A few years ago, Karl was constructing a rock wall, but he was hampered by a bad back. It should come as no surprise that Rachel took over the job and saw it through to completion.

"The trick is to roll the rocks, not lift them. I read up on it and found that's the way our forefathers did it," she says.

After building walkways, walls, and steps of rock and brick, she has even grown fond of this hefty art.

"When you finish a rock wall, you look at the mass of the thing and you know you really accomplished something. I've read that Winston Churchill laid bricks as a hobby. If it's good enough for Winston, it's good enough for me," she says.

Balancing her hard-edged accomplishments, Rachel also tackles a host of traditional homemaking tasks with creativity. An avid cook, she has taken courses in the preparation of chocolate, and how to

Above left: Rachel ages her Choctaw baskets by dipping them in a dark stain she concocts from black walnuts. Above right: A bevy of baskets, boxes, and trays on display. Soap cakes can be seen in the foreground.

make the most of Mexican, French, Chinese, and Indian cuisines. She also keeps up to a dozen sheep on her farm for those times when she needs wool or fresh soap. None of this is a burden.

"My family goes back to the Mayflower, so I've always had an interest in American crafts and the old ways of doing things. But we're lucky enough to live in a time when we have a lot of laborsaving devices for cooking, cleaning, and building. I don't face the drudgery that my ancestors did. I can have fun without so much of the hard work," she says.

As a beneficiary of Rachel's talents, Karl says he has grown to realize how gifted his wife actually is.

"With her tremendous energy, she's always busy doing something beautiful and wonderful for our home. It makes me feel guilty when I just want to relax and watch a football game," he says.

But she certainly isn't trying to stir up guilt or steal the limelight for herself. She simply wants to create an atmosphere for fine living.

"A person can make a good impression with the smallest thing. For instance, I've taken five years of basket-making classes. So, when we go to someone's house, I always take along a basket I've made for them, rather than a bottle of wine or something I've purchased. People always seem so surprised and pleased," she says.

It's the kind of gesture anyone could offer.

"All you have to do is sign up for a class." □

Above: *To get rocks up an incline like this, Rachel rolls them over a plank using a sturdy steel rod for leverage. "I learned to build stone walls just by doing. You put the pieces together like a puzzle— and you have a beautiful wall," she says.*

Right: *Rachel watches as her sheep graze in the Van Leer meadow near Valley Pond. "Though we're only a dozen miles from downtown Boston, living here is like being in Vermont," she says.*

THE SWEET HERBAL AIRS OF

Gabler's Farm

By Candace Ord Manroe

Mary Ella Gabler imagined many possibilities for herself in life. One she did not consider was starring in a real-life reenactment of the old television sitcom Green Acres.

That's the role she was cast when her husband, Ray, a Dallas businessman nostalgic for the southern Texas cotton farm of his boyhood, determined to get a country place of his own.

Like Eddie Albert's Oliver, Ray was out to transform a proverbial sow's-ear farmhouse into a charming—and herb-filled—silk purse. ✿

Photographs: Hickey-Robertson

❋

He would eventually turn the country place into an herb-growing business called Gabler's Farm—and Mary Ella would be his partner.

It's not that she was a neophyte at bucolic living. Mary Ella grew up in the Pennsylvania countryside but had come a long way from the farm. Stints as a New York stockbroker and owner of a bedding shop in the fashionable Park Cities of Dallas left her little resolve for things primitive.

Eva Gabor's *Green Acres* lament—"I just adore a penthouse view!"—haunted her; reluctantly, inevitably, she found herself in the same role.

In all fairness to Ray, he didn't march straight from the couple's home in the Park Cities to his own version of *Green Acres*. In between, he restored a Victorian home in Granbury, Texas, that he and Mary Ella used as a weekend escape. Granbury, only about 70 miles from Dallas, was a quick commute and offered the pristine charms of a

Previous page: *Ray and Mary Ella Gabler added wraparound porches to their 100-year-old Acton, Texas, farmhouse, also shown above right.*
Left: *Antique wicker and a rustic bench built by Ray's father combine happily with sophisticated fabrics.*

turn-of-the-century Texas town, with limestone courthouse and town square.

But it didn't gratify Ray's hankering for land. Just outside Granbury, in the countryside known as Acton, he stumbled across 54 acres of Brazos River bottomland. A creek cut a gentle swath through the property, and a giant live oak shaded what was left of an early farmhouse.

Mary Ella hesitates to call the building, as it then existed, a house.

"It had big holes in the roof, a crumbling fireplace, no screens or doors, and it was filled with an abundance of copperheads, opossums, raccoons, rats, scorpions, dirt dobbers, and rattlesnakes. When Ray saw this place he fell in love with the land and bought it. I wouldn't go in it for eight months," she recalls.

Left: *Rustic meets refined in the living room, where walls are an unlikely combination of soft fabrics, washed-cedar wainscoting, and half-round bleached cedar beams. All work was executed by Jay Horner, an Acton carpenter.*
Top right: *Leading directly into the living room, the front porch invites an appreciation for the easy life.*
Bottom right: *Texas vignettes such as this grouping of cowboy hats (actually worn by Ray) dot the living room.*

❖

Ray admits the old clapboard structure wasn't exactly cozy or accommodating.

"There was no plumbing, and all the electrical wiring was faulty and deteriorated. The water well was dry," he says.

But Ray, now confident in his restoration abilities, envisioned an authentic early Texas farmhouse whose appeal would rest in its earnest simplicity and stolid comforts such as a wraparound porch, which he would have to add.

Except for the porch addition, lines of the 100-year-old architecture were left unaltered. No frilly gingerbread trims, no flashy exterior paint combinations sullied the idea of the house as it looked when first constructed. After structural improvements were made, the house was painted white, suggestive of an inevitable bleaching process by the harsh Texas sun.

The idea of regional purity carries forth into the interior, too: Dining room walls were stripped to

Left: *Lace-paneled French doors bring an outdoor ambience into the shiplap-walled dining room.* Right: *Painted a bold, unexpected persimmon-burgundy, barn board transforms the small kitchen into one of the most delightful spaces.*

❀

expose the home's original shiplap construction.

When design decisions became a matter of historical accuracy versus creativity, creativity was the easy victor.

They covered the small kitchen's walls in barn board then departed from the typical farmhouse tableau by painting them an electrifying persimmon-burgundy.

Ralph Lauren's Country Store in New York City inspired the living room's design. Walls were covered with washed-cedar wainscoting, and cedar half-round beams were built on the upper walls and ceiling. The rustic structural beams are perched against incongruously elegant backgrounds of fabric.

With the renovation complete, Ray was ready to relax and enjoy the place. An enthusiastic cook, he planted an herb garden to facilitate these culinary adventures.

But Ray's business acumen told him there was more to his garden than what ended up on his tabletop. The sandy soil of the river basin was ideal for growing not just a few common herbs, but a range of exotic herbs, greens, and baby vegetables.

Gabler's Farm soon was a thriving business, supplying chefs at premiere Dallas restaurants and, recently, even one in New York City.

These days, the farm works better than even Ray imagined. It's a source of revenue and greater riches: the hours Ray and Mary Ella spend together rocking on the wraparound porch beneath a crimson Texas sunset, the scent of herbs hanging sweetly in the air.□

Left: *The master bedroom is a study in romance with antique linens and bedding from Mary Ella's shop. A porcelain bovine, a touch of Texana, guards a bedside table.*
Right: *A judicious use of fabric and regional accents such as the hatstand add interest to the home's small guest bedroom.*

·PENCHANT FOR·
PERMANENCE

By Steve Cooper. Produced by Estelle Bond Guralnick

Rhode Islander Builds Tradition

Home builder Michael Blanchflower's first brief career as a Rhode Island state police officer lasted only four years.

"I'd find myself looking at buildings while I was out on patrol: studying the different styles, thinking about the way I'd build things. It slowly dawned on me that I might be happier putting up houses than enforcing laws," Michael says.

He was particularly intrigued by structures still standing after two centuries or more. In a hasty, production-line age, Michael was attracted to their elegance, sturdiness, and permanence.

"I like a place where I stand inside and get the feeling that, though I might not be here a hundred years from now, this house will be. You can find them throughout New England. Houses that have stood up to

Opposite: *The first house Michael Blanchflower built was his own. Like his colonial predecessors, he worked only with hand tools. "I did the whole house with a hand plane and I paid for it. I was worn out all the time. Power tools aren't such a bad idea," he says.* Above, *Michael with Karen, his wife, and children, Jessica and Michael.*

Photographs: Julie Maris/Semel

The building process sometimes begins as a contemplative exercise in the forest. Michael moves among pines, oaks, and other trees looking for timbers growing strong and straight. He carefully picks those suitable to their stressful tasks.

"I need a couple of dozen trees for a house. But it's getting so hard to find good timbers, it doesn't pay for me to go out and find the trees any longer unless they're right on the property. Lately I've been buying trees from local logging companies," he says.

Michael accompanies a logger into the woods to cut timbers, below. *Once beams are shaped, he creates details using both power tools and hand tools. He chisels out a notch,* bottom.

"Power tools may speed things up. But for finish work, nothing can replace a hammer, a chisel, and a pair of hands," he says.

• PENCHANT FOR PERMANENCE •

everything winter could throw," he says.

The secret to such longevity is a matter of inner strength. These houses were erected around frames made of heavy posts and beams. The future was fixed to 8-inch-square timbers stretching 20 feet and more.

After apprenticing under an experienced timber framer, Michael launched his own business nine years ago. His résumé was his own home, a 17th-century reproduction in Harrisville.

Karen Blanchflower says her husband always knew exactly what he wanted.

"Before he ever began, he had it all planned right down to what the curtains would look like and what kind of forks and spoons he would use. He's unusually talented, and he never settles for anything less than he wants," she says.

Opposite: Michael put up the beams, laid the rock fireplace, hammered down the floor, and built the table in the keeping room. Above: If he could change one thing, it might be the upstairs bedroom floors. "They're just planks. No subfloor. No sound insulation. Sometimes it sounds like the kids are jackhammering up there," he says.

A stone's throw from Michael's house is his small mill, where he transforms rough logs into beams and lumber. He installed the one-man operation under a tin roof in 1978 for a very bottom-line reason.

"Every time I went to buy lumber, the price had jumped. So I started looking around for a used mill. You can find them all over New England. Not long ago, I saw where 144 old mills were operating in Rhode Island alone," he says.

His Lane mill is little different from a model built at the turn of the century. A stationary tractor engine powers a 52-inch blade. It's strong enough to rip the softest pine or tough-as-nails oak.

"If I'm whittling down big logs, I might have to stop once or twice a day to sharpen the blade; at least that often if I'm working oak. It's hard work, but I never have to wait or pay someone else's prices," he says.

He saws beams as thick as 21 inches or planks as thin as a quarter-inch.

·PENCHANT FOR PERMANENCE·
Colonial Comforts

It was love at first sight for Michael. "The first time I saw a post-and-beam house, I knew that was what I wanted. Later, I discovered how many people feel the same way," he says.

He learned the trade as an apprentice to experienced builder Armond Lamontagne.

"I was driving down the street one day when I saw three reproduction houses he was working on. I was intrigued by all those beams laid out on the ground, so I stopped to talk. Well, I'd never seen anything like that and pretty soon I was out there working with him, copying him," Michael says.

A similar process brought Michael his first clients. He was working on his own house when people stopped, watching him hoisting beams and carving out joints. Soon, he was contracted to do a house. When that house was complete, it caught the fancy of a couple who became Michael's second commission. A career was born.

For years, Richard and Marcia Tramonti admired the home of early American portrait artist Gilbert Stuart. It took another artist, Michael Blanchflower, to make the dream a reality.

"Michael is a very gifted young man. He's a craftsman in a time when that's rare," Marcia says.

The house was built from Rhode Island pine by Michael and a single helper in 1984.

"Our home is a quiet haven that embraces us with comfort and peace. It is a step back in time," Marcia says.

Opposite: *With its broad, open first floor, Marcia and Richard Tramonti's home is an entertaining space conducive to successful dinner parties. "We enjoy entertaining, and the open floor plan on the first level allows for my guests to all participate. Our gatherings are warm and cordial," Marcia says.* Above: *The Tramontis.*

Hand-Built Homestead

Michael invests about a month preparing a timber frame. Though their design seems as simple as a child's toy construction kit, each piece must be precisely crafted for its specific duty. An engineer's detailing is applied as each timber is sawed, planed, carved, and formed for joining, below. "When it's ready to go, I bring a crane on-site for a day and put up the frame. That's the most exciting day. In a matter of hours, the outline of the house takes shape," Michael says.

As he hammers on floors, siding, and a roof, the emerging house combines old and new.

"I hope people like what they see from the outside. I want them to catch a glimpse of the 17th or 18th century. But I also hope that people who live in my houses really enjoy them. They aren't meant to be museum pieces. They're meant to be lived in by modern families with a modern way of living."

For Ed and Paula Short, post-and-beam construction is more than a link with the past. It's also a way to enjoy the present.

"With post-and-beam we could eliminate interior walls. Because we have so much glass, the house has a very open, airy feel. It's not quite authentic to the period, but it's comfortable. We love it," Paula says.

The couple's Pascoag, Rhode Island, home was built by Michael Blanchflower in 1983.

"Michael really cares about everything he does. He's an artist, and houses are his medium," says Paula. □

Opposite: *"What Michael built was our dream house,"* says Paula Short. *A flood of light from glass doors along the southern wall gives the Shorts' great-room contemporary appeal in a traditional Cape Cod-style setting.* Above: *Ed and Paula Short with son, Chas. A daughter, Alexandra, was born after this photo was taken.*

IN THE SHADOW OF THE CITY

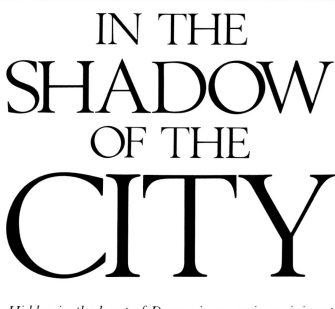

Hidden in the heart of Denver is an oasis reminiscent of the English countryside: a tiny two-story cottage surrounded by lush and informal gardens that overflow with flowers, vegetables, and herbs.

IN THE
SHADOW
OF THE
CITY

By Molly Culbertson

A small Victorian near downtown
Denver is nestled into quaint
gardens that seem to keep the urban
hustle at bay. Here, flowers overgrow
their beds, vegetables ripen on stalk
and vine, and herbs grow everywhere
something else doesn't.

The scene belies its surroundings,
for this is one of Denver's oldest and
most densely populated
neighborhoods. The simple house and
lusty gardens—all neatly contained
within a white picket fence—might
seem more at home in some sylvan
setting than at city's center. But
homeowner Rob Proctor, an artist,
garden writer, and botanical
illustrator, wanted a property that
would reflect the casual style of the
English countryside.

He and fellow garden enthusiast
David Macke began creating that
look by planting flowers in muted
colors that blend together; warm
pastels contrast with cooler ones. The
layout of the gardens is formal, and
includes a complex raised bed—a
25 × 35-foot network of eight beds in
a figure eight design. But there the
formality ends; the gardeners prefer
the softer look of freely growing

Opposite: *Wicker furnishes the back patio
of Rob Proctor's small home near
downtown Denver.*
Above right: *Lilies, Rob's favorite flowers,
bloom throughout the gardens.*
Near right: *The back porch is a workroom
for handling the harvest of flowers, herbs,
and vegetables.*
Far right: *Rob tends vining plants that
grow behind the house.*

Photographs: Michael Jensen
Produced by Jill Carey-Mordini

flora. "We've planted the beds informally," Rob says. "They're put together like the colors of a Monet painting—at least I hope so."

The gardens come to life in March, when tiny crocuses and anemones work their way through the last of the snow. In April, 2,000 bulbs begin their bloom: tulips, daffodils, snow irises, fritillarias, alliums, and hyacinths. Soon such old-fashioned perennials as peonies, primroses, and polemoniums begin to open their buds; later in the summer, their colors are replaced by a profusion of lilies and clematis. White-blooming plants are woven throughout to help highlight other colors.

Flowers bloom until the end of the season—usually early October. "I buy new plantings all through the summer," Rob says. "Anytime I see anything that looks interesting, I put it in—wherever I need a fresh burst of color." Where there are no garden beds, he's filled terra-cotta pots with geraniums, petunias, lobelias, begonias, impatiens, holly, dwarf gladioli, lilies, coleus, and ferns.

Late afternoon is the best time to enjoy the gardens, Rob says. Many blossoms, including flowering tobacco and night-scented stock, are most fragrant when the sun loses its

Above left: *Garden benches are arranged all over the property, inviting visitors to sit and enjoy the sights and scents of the gardens.*
Opposite top *and* near right: *The home's interior is filled with primitive antiques— finds from flea markets, estate sales, and junking excursions.*
Far right: *The 1886 house is a simple structure the owners chose because it allowed them to express their own styles. "It didn't seem to dictate that we conform to a particular period," David Macke says.*

IN THE
SHADOW
OF THE
CITY

intensity, and the soft blue, white, light yellow, and pale pink blooms show up well in the setting sun.

Two years ago, Rob and David expanded the garden space by digging a bed for vegetables and herbs next door. Now the 50×100-foot area, once a city parking lot, provides a bounty that Rob begs friends to help consume: tomatoes, squash, broccoli, corn, spinach, beans, and beets, plus some 50 species of culinary and aromatic herbs.

When weather did not permit outdoor chores, attention was directed toward refurbishing the small house. Built in 1886, the two-story structure has little of the ornateness typical of Victorian architecture. Its simplicity, however, is part of the house's appeal: It happily accommodates an eclectic assortment of collections and furnishings. The result is a style that Rob describes as part farmhouse, part town house.

The back porch is the most used room in the house, for it's here that most of the gardens' harvest is handled—the cut flowers arranged, herbs readied for drying, and vegetables prepared for preservation. Shelves are filled with garden tools, seed catalogs, and cookbooks.

Opposite: *Terra-cotta pots and baskets are filled with foliage plants and blooming annuals to add color even where there are no garden beds.*
Above right: *A pair of stained-glass windows now hang in the door frame between the dining room and living room. Here and throughout the house, Oriental carpets contrast with primitive pine antiques.*
Right: *Collectibles on display include toy horses, stoneware, and old basketry. Rob's landscape paintings and botanicals hang on the walls.*

Other rooms are dressier. Walls are papered in soft floral patterns, woodwork is painted in gleaming white, and floors are lined with Oriental carpets.

Most of the furnishings here are primitive, however, and most, like the collectibles, have been gleaned from flea markets and junking excursions. The pine dining table was found in an abandoned miner's cabin in Montana, for example; the assortment of ladder-back chairs came from various antiques shops. A Mennonite cupboard displays blue-and-white china and English stoneware pudding molds; crockery lines the shelves of a colonial corner cabinet. In every room are flower-filled baskets and old toy horses.

On the walls is evidence of Rob's background in fine art: the watercolor landscapes and botanical illustrations he paints during the winter months (or whenever inclement weather keeps him from his gardens).

"Some people might consider this a lot of work," Rob says of the maintenance of his prolific gardens, "but work is what you do when you'd rather be doing something else. And there's nothing else I'd rather be doing." □

Above: Rob allows the perennials to grow freely against the white picket fence. The result is a slightly wild garden that would be at home in the English countryside.

August

Country Home

Borne to Blues

Friendship Cabin

Piece by Piece

Untamed Paradise

Above: *Built in 1900 as a summer lodge, the Borne home is situated
on a wooded acre across the Mississippi River from the New Orleans French Quarter.*
Opposite: *Barry and Brenda Borne, with their black Labrador retriever, Crockett,
enjoy country life in the heart of the city.*

BORNE TO *Blues*

Designer Brenda Borne and her husband, Barry, love the softer side of color. Their 90-year-old New Orleans home is a harmony of basic blues.

By Bonnie Warren with Candace Ord Manroe

Among its other distinctions, New Orleans' French Quarter is recognized as the home of the blues. Directly across the Mississippi River, in the historic town of Algiers (now a part of the city), stands another tribute to blues: the home of designer Brenda Borne and her husband, Barry.

Their two-story home, origi-nally known as Donner Lodge when it was built as a rambling summer cottage for a wealthy family in 1900, went through a succession of own-ers. Each added to or altered the floor plan; by the time the Bornes bought the house, a major redo was in order.

"We loved the basic charac-ter of the house," Brenda says,

Photographs: David Richmond. Produced with Ann Omvig Manternach.

"but we wanted to give it a country flavor."

Adding liberal helpings of their personal tastes, such as a proclivity for the color blue, the Bornes set about returning their historic home to its original character. The history of the Algiers neighborhood was too rich, they reasoned, for one of its grand Victorians not to be an authentic reflection of the past.

Algiers originally was called King's Plantation. The founder of New Orleans, Jean-Baptiste Le Moyne Bienville, chose Algiers over New Orleans as his own home in the early 1700s. Even Adrien de Pauger, the chief engineer who designed the original plan for the French Quarter, claimed a pie-shaped piece of Algiers as his own.

In time the land was divided and a quaint town flourished. Victorian houses with gingerbread trim dotted the narrow streets. Access to New Orleans was provided by a ferry. Historians described Algiers as a small town with a semirural atmosphere.

By 1900, New Orleans folks were crossing the river in search of a quieter place. Algiers was the perfect choice with its lush greenery and tall moss-draped oaks.

So it was that the Bornes' home was built. Donner Lodge was the talk of New Orleans: It

Opposite: *Wood casting molds for ship gears found during an early morning stroll on the nearby Mississippi River levee stand out boldly against one of the living room's blue walls.* Above: *A collection of white linens grouped over the living room couch adds a soft touch of nostalgia to the blue-and-white theme. French doors lead to a porch, where morning coffee is enjoyed.*

BORNE TO *Blues*

had both Algiers' first swimming pool and its first tennis court.

But the Bornes were more interested in restoring charm than status to the home after purchasing it in 1979. First on the list of changes was dismantling the 1950s kitchen.

"We ripped everything out and installed a homey 1920s-style country kitchen," says Brenda. She designed the custom-built white cabinets to appear old, even down to just the right hardware, which is reminiscent of that on Brenda's prized turn-of-the-century Hoosier baking cupboard.

The comfortable floor plan is anything but the predictable two-story pattern. The dining room is downstairs, yet the living room is upstairs. It all makes perfect sense, however, since the living room takes full advantage of the wide second-level porch, and the dining room adjoins the downstairs kitchen, which was once the caretaker's quarters.

As well as the kitchen and formal dining room, the downstairs includes a sun-room, den or great-room with a fireplace, bathroom, and laundry room. Upstairs, there are two bedrooms, a study, and a bathroom, in addition to the living room and porch.

Above: *Antique needlepoint pillows on the den/great-room's love seat illustrate Brenda's attention to quality, even in the details.*
Opposite: *The dining room furniture and tableware are family antiques.*
Above right: *Brenda refreshed the den's dark paneling by painting it white.*

"The plan is especially good for entertaining," Brenda says. "The downstairs flows together so well we even had more than two hundred people here for my niece's wedding reception without feeling crowded."

Features, such as the dining room adjoining the kitchen through French doors, contribute to the home's easy flow. Large windows in the sun-room bring the outside in on the rear of the house, and a door opens to spacious grounds with huge moss-draped oaks and magnolias.

The Wedgwood blue of the exterior, with pristine white accents, is repeated throughout the house. "Blue is restful," Brenda explains, "and I was still able to introduce other colors."

Although Brenda is the professional interior designer of the family, Barry was involved in every step of the home's transformation. "We did most of the work ourselves," he says, "and I helped Brenda scour antiques stores for the right furniture and accessories."

One of the most interesting additions to the house came during one of the Bornes' early morning walks along the nearby Mississippi River levee that overlooks the French Quarter. "I found the wooden die-casting molds washed up on the levee bank," Brenda says.

BORNE TO Blues

"She made me drag them home and clean them up for the stairwell," adds Barry.

"We also frequented flea markets looking for some of the old things we have used throughout the house," Brenda says. "However, the sign in the kitchen—'Borne's Hardware'—is a special treasure since it's from Barry's family's old store in Algiers," she says.

Despite her vocation, Brenda places little stock in the thought of furnishing a home with any great speed—or through just a few shops. "It takes patience to shop for furnishings and accessories, but the reward is well worth the effort. For example, it took us almost five years to find our beloved Hoosier cabinet, and we searched for three and a half years to locate just the right lamp for the living room," explains Brenda.

Brenda is never quite settled about the interior of the house but enjoys the flexibility of periodically changing and rearranging.

"First, I had the dining room where the sunroom is now." She adds, smiling, "Barry is very patient."

However, it did take months of persuasion to get Barry to agree to paint the den white. "The paneling was dark brown," Brenda recalls. "Barry said he liked it just fine, thank

Above and opposite: The Bornes replaced the 1950s kitchen with a 1920s look. Their new kitchen cabinets were made to blend with the style of Brenda's beloved turn-of-the-century Indiana Hoosier baking cupboard. Right: French doors from the dining room open onto the kitchen's breakfast area.

you. But I finally won, and now he likes the white walls and ceiling."

The couple worked together to create the lush surrounding garden. "We originally fell in love with the acre of land," Brenda says. "However, it takes a great deal of time to keep everything looking just right."

The charming rock fence and iron gates have always been a part of the setting. The raised swimming pool now seems a bit outdated, but it is in perfect working order and there are no plans to change it. The tennis court that, along with the pool, originally brought local fame to the summer estate no longer exists, however. A charming fish pond now occupies its place.

Brenda and Barry had no trouble meeting their contemporary needs within the confines of an old look. Even their garage fits beautifully into the country setting. It is built to look more like a barn than a garage, with white-trim cross posts on the large doors.

The Bornes are anything but blythe about owning the old Donner Lodge. They know exactly what they've got and how lucky they are to have it.

"We enjoy sitting on the porch swing with a cup of coffee and relaxing," Barry says. "It really is hard to realize that we are actually a part

Top: *Brenda's great-grandmother made the antique quilt covering the bed in the guest room overlooking the second-story front porch.*
Above: *White café curtains with lace trim cover the windows in the back bedroom, formerly a sleeping porch. Brenda and Barry use this as their master bedroom.*

of the city now. Living in this place feels exactly like being out in the country."

That was precisely the effect that Barry and Brenda wanted, inevitable urban sprawl notwithstanding.

Today, Algiers bears few traces from its formative years as King's Plantation. It has grown to a population of more than 30,000 and has been incorporated into Orleans Parish, or New Orleans. The Bornes' home is one of only a few early houses that remain; newer look-alike houses have encroached on the old summer estates in the name of progress.

Instead of having to travel aboard ferry to reach the Bornes' house, as in its halcyon Donner Lodge days, all that's necessary today is making the speedy drive across one of twin bridges that span the three miles to the east bank of the Mississippi River.

Still, once at the home, the sense of yesteryear is strong—made even stronger, perhaps, by all the surrounding change.

"This is an oasis," insists Brenda. "We live a relaxed life much like the original owners envisioned. The difference is we don't have to travel to the country to do it," she says. □

Friendship Cabin

When constructed in 1840, this chestnut cabin below had two full stories—filled by 10 children. In 1988, Gloria and Joe Sewell bought the guest cabin and had it moved from Tennessee to their home in Canton, Georgia.

By Candace Ord Manroe. Produced by Ruth Reiter

Schoolchildren loved watching Gloria Sewell spin wool and dip candles. But lugging her paraphernalia to demonstrations was wearing. The solution: move a log cabin behind her home, and the children could come to her. In the same spirit of friendship, the cabin would be home to houseguests, too.

Above: *Birdhouses scattered among perennials set the tone for a nature walk around the cabin, through woods and wildflowers.*

Right: *The kitchen is a new addition built to the rear of the cabin in the old lean-to style. The mid-1800s table is from southern Georgia.*

𝒻riendship Cabin

Above: *An avid gardener, homeowner Gloria Sewell has been challenged by the cabin's site in a shady hollow.*

"I do very useful things," deadpans Gloria Sewell.

"I can spin, but I can't knit. If you need thread, I can make it, but I can't sew on your button. I also can dip candles, but there isn't much demand."

Gloria's old-fashioned skills admittedly aren't as serviceable today as they would have been in colonial times. But her protean repertoire from the past, which even includes hearth cooking, did earn Gloria considerable popularity as a guest speaker at area schools. And it is this fact which, in a roundabout way, is responsible for the log cabin now gracing her and her husband Joe's home in Canton, Georgia.

"It got to the point where I was constantly loading and unloading my car because of so many demonstrations to school groups," remembers Gloria.

She didn't want to give up the opportunity to share with children, who had evinced a real interest in her lectures. But the hassle with logistics—hauling cumbersome tools and dressing in period costume—was too much.

"One solution was to bring the children to me, but I needed a place at my home where I could accommodate them," explains Gloria.

She and Joe had always loved early log cabins. If they could move one to their property, they reasoned, it would be the perfect environment for demonstrating colonial crafts and cooking.

Not only that, but the cabin also could serve as a warm, private guesthouse for out-of-town friends.

Photographs: Rick Taylor.

Entertaining could also acquire a new flavor within old chinked walls.

The Sewells retained professional cabin restorer Dave Howard to begin the search for the right cabin, which he soon located in Claiborne County, Tennessee.

Built in 1840 of chestnut logs, it offered everything the Sewells wanted: adequate space, primitive beauty, and a lively history. Originally, the cabin spanned two stories and was home to a couple with 10 children. That kind of track record, Gloria knew, would suit her purposes fine; visiting schoolchildren would fit right in.

Howard moved the cabin to Georgia, then carefully re-assembled it in a hollow below the Sewells' main house.

"At first, I was an absolute purist. I didn't want anything done to the cabin that wasn't authentic," says Gloria. "But when I thought about thirty children in it at one time, with no bathroom, I reconsidered."

A new section was built onto the rear to accommodate a full bathroom and a kitchen. A new front porch and roof were added, and the interior was redesigned to reduce the full two stories to one story and a sleeping loft, with tall ceilings elsewhere.

Once the cabin made structural sense for their needs, Gloria and Joe were respectful of its age and integrity. Instead of chinking the logs with only a mixture of portland cement and sand, the Sewells had buff coloring added for a more natural look. All rock underpinning for the cabin was gathered right off their property—the same method that would have been used 150 years ago.

Above: *Originally closed, the stairway facing the living room was opened up by Gloria and Joe to expose more of the cabin's log interior and to emit more natural light downstairs.*

Opposite: *The two-story fireplace is the main room's focal point, defined by a pair of wing chairs, a 100-year-old quilt, and some of Gloria's collection of fireplace cookware. Flooring is new pine, stained and polyurethaned to withstand heavy wear.*

Friendship Cabin

117

Opposite: *In the front corner of the living room, much as it would have been in the 1800s, is one of Gloria's favorite pieces—a "hired man's" bed. The cabin dollhouse is old—probably made by a father for his daughter.*

Left: *Another of Gloria's special antiques is a homemade child's bed with rubbed edges and ropes across the top to hold the blanket in place over a sleeping child. She prizes it because "it is so honest." The horse and cupboard both are old.*

Below: *Gloria kept the sleeping loft simple with an old iron bed, blanket chest, and rocker. Originally, the upstairs would have been strewn with straw pallets for children.*

Care was taken to meld the new kitchen addition with the existing structure as unobtrusively as possible. The most convincing approach was a lean-to—what the original owners probably would've built had they needed more space. Walls and floors were kept simple, too, with plain pine boards.

Furnishing the cabin involved some shopping at antiques stores for appropriate country pieces. However, because Gloria's fondness for rustic American antiques already was well established before the cabin was purchased, furnishing also was a matter of dipping into her existing collections.

Since obtaining the cabin two years ago, Gloria has developed even more uses for it than she originally envisioned. "I put in a nature trail that's about a half mile long, full of wildflowers," she says. She also has established a perennial garden in front of the cabin. School groups enjoy taking the nature trail—but so do the Sewells and their houseguests.

The cabin itself has been a tremendous hit for those lucky enough to spend time there. "Our friends who come to stay who haven't seen the cabin before are very surprised and delighted. I think they have one thing in mind when they hear 'log cabin'—and they find this to be something very different," says Gloria. "They always seem to love it."

And for Gloria and Joe, sharing the cabin with friends and children is the real joy of ownership. □

riendship Cabin

Piece by Piece

Quilt dealer Rick Snyder traded a suit-and-tie career for the life of collecting he's always loved.

Right: Colorful majolica sets an inviting scene. Above: Rick Snyder began collecting in his teens. Below: Restoration uncovered gingerbread in near perfect condition.

While other teenagers dropped spare cash on record albums and pepperoni pizzas, Rick Snyder was packing his mother's spare bedroom to the ceiling with antique quilts he'd bought at auctions.

Even at the ripe age of 16, Rick had a keen eye for collectibles and a gutsy business sense. It didn't take a high school counselor to predict that Rick would end up specializing in antique quilts and restoring vintage homes.

"I had gone to five or six auctions and seen quilts sell and just got to thinking about it," Rick says. "Something just clicked. I raised my hand and bought a twenty-two-dollar wedding-ring quilt in perfect condition. From then on, I spent every dime I ever saved or ever made on antique quilts. That's what set me up in the quilt business."

Rick landed in Eureka Springs in 1980. Lured from a traditional job with a Fortune 500 company, Rick fell in love with the creative energy in Eureka Springs. Shops up and down the main thoroughfare burst with antiques and traditional Ozark crafts. Beautifully restored Victorian mansions and cottages lined the streets. Like thousands before him, Rick decided to make this unusual place his home.

Rick opened a small quilt shop downtown, moving after one year to a larger store down the street. (Later he renovated yet another store.) Then his attention turned to homes. Rick bought and restored three places before settling into

 Photographs: William N. Hopkins, Hopkins Associates. Regional editor: Mary Anne Thomson

Piece by Piece

his current Queen Anne Victorian. It was his eye for a good antique that saw potential in the charming, albeit neglected, home.

Rick found the house smothered in asbestos siding. Hardwood floors hid beneath outdated carpet. Poor planning divided the back half of the house into a tiny kitchen, bedroom, and bath. Yellow metal cabinets lined the kitchen walls, and accoustical tile covered the ceiling.

The house was built in the town's turn-of-the-century prime by a local druggist. He was one of the many who benefited from Eureka Springs' claim to a wellspring of healing water. Hundreds of similar homes—complete with wraparound porches and fancy trims—sprang up along the narrow winding streets between 1880 and 1910. Dozens of contractors were needed to keep up with the demand for houses and shops. Today, residents restore these homes with equal fervor.

"It took about nine months to remodel, but I lived across the street," Rick says. "I had no idea all the gingerbread was under there. It was in perfect condition. I have always had a lot of respect for this home."

Rick set to work transforming the typically narrow rooms into wide-open spaces. The hardwood floors reappeared. White paint brightened the interior, and the upstairs attic was converted into a bedroom suite.

Rick gutted the whole back end of the house, sweeping away the dingy kitchen and replacing it with an open, homey area for cooking and socializing. At last Rick had a house large enough to display his many collections, and to catch the runover of quilts from his shop downtown. Today, a bow window opens up the view to the woods just beyond the yard. A stone path marks the way to a tiny cottage that Rick built for guests.

The kitchen flows into the dining room where Rick hangs antique prints, quilts, and his bonnet and sampler collections. The double living room is light and airy, warmed by a cozy fireplace and an ever-changing mix of collectibles. Guests escape to the back bedroom, which opens onto a sunny porch retreat.

Left: Carefully selected bargains fill Rick's home. The 1880s painted chair was found in Missouri for $3. Metal antique cars and stuffed animals are sprinkled randomly throughout the house. Below: The faux-grained pine dresser displays a collection of antique Santas. A 1920s quilt covers the turn-of-the-century bed.

Piece by Piece

Far right: *Rick found the couch and easy chair abandoned on roadsides. A fresh covering of upholstery transformed them both.*

Right: *These old stuffed rabbits are inspiration for reproduction pieces that Rick commissions for his store. The samplers are takeoffs from antiques.*

Below: *Teddy bears and samplers guide the way to the upstairs suite. The bear collection began 10 years ago after Rick confided to a family member that he'd never owned one as a child.*

Every room holds hidden treasures: Stoneware bowls, crib quilts, antique glass, vintage toys, and painted pieces.

"My taste is very eclectic. I don't collect anything in particular, just everything," Rick says. His decorating style reflects the same flexibility and emotional appeal. Tramp art shares space with antique quilts, jars of marbles, button collections,

and metal tricycles. There's no rhyme or reason to where things go. (His cleaning help claims to find some of the best combinations.)

Many of his collections began as gifts. One friend noticed a couple of bonnets on his wall, so every year she gave him another antique bonnet. Voilà! A new collection was born.

"I don't read books on what the value of things are," Rick says. "If things look handmade and loved and worn, that's what I like. That's what I buy."

Rick's willingness to venture into unusual territory has produced some amazing finds. Most of his upholstered furniture has led a ragtag life. Rick calls them road finds—interesting furniture that he has scavenged from curbside garbage piles.

"I'll be driving along and see these wonderful pieces of furniture that somebody's tossed out, and I can't bear it," Rick says.

This quirky knack for resurrection abounds in Eureka Springs. Like Rick, many people operate stores during the tourist season, run B&Bs from their homes throughout the year, and restore real estate in whatever spare time remains.

"It's just the style of life that I like," says Rick. "I've worn the suits, the white shirts, and the ties. I'm just not into that. Eureka Springs is like being on vacation twelve months of the year." □

Right: *"Allow time to enjoy your creation,"
says watercolorist and gardener Elizabeth
Crookham. Throughout the property are
chairs and benches where the artist and
her husband, Charles, can read or reflect.*

Far right: *Elizabeth's cat, Horace
Rumpole, enjoys the view from the front
step of the Crookhams' 1940s Cape Cod.
Lining the walk are candytufts and
columbines; in pots are geraniums,
impatiens, begonias, and petunias.*

UNTAMED
Paradise
An Artist's Inspiration

❦

A watercolorist has transformed her Portland, Oregon, property into an urban wilderness—a garden retreat that lures her to her easel throughout the season.

By Molly Culbertson
Produced by Cathy Howard

Settled in her home on a Portland hillside, Elizabeth Crookham surrounds herself with her favorite art media—watercolors and flowers. Her splendid gardens, now in their seventh season, bear testimony to Elizabeth's love of color as well as to her attentiveness.

With a careful assortment of early- to late-blooming perennials, Elizabeth manages to keep the gardens looking always at their peak, bursting with color from late in the winter through the end of fall. In return, they

Above: *Elizabeth's garden is informal but not haphazard: She's given much consideration to flower colors and shapes, adding new plantings and moving perennials from bed to bed each season.*

Right: *A careful combination of flowers packed into nearly every available space ensures color from late winter to late fall.*

Above: *This slightly wild corner of the Crookhams' garden is typical of the look Elizabeth has created by choosing flowers based on their colors and shapes.*

Right: *Behind the house, Elizabeth grows flowers in raised beds. It's a kind of test garden, where she can see the color and form of a new variety one season before planting it in the front garden the next.*

Right: *Behind their house, Elizabeth and Charles put in a 35-foot square terrace that adjoins their dining and living rooms. They planted the area with native trees and shrubs, azaleas, clematis and honeysuckle, and hydrangeas. Elizabeth filled pots with colorful annuals and perennials so that she can move color wherever she wants it.*

UNTAMED

Paradise

provide infinite inspiration for her floral watercolor paintings.

The 1940s Cape Cod where Elizabeth and her husband, Charles, have lived for more than 30 years provides a picturesque backdrop for the vibrant gardens. Elizabeth wanted to create an illusion of greater space here, where the house stands quite close to the street. She decided dense growth would do that: She planted flowering cherry trees and a row of perennials curbside, had a split-rail fence built at the sidewalk, and filled the remaining lawn with flowers. No grass remains—Elizabeth prefers tending the flowers to mowing grass.

The beds are planted informally and designed for low maintenance. It's intentionally not tidy, Elizabeth explains. Friends think hers is an English-style garden, she says, "but I think English peo-ple would be horrified. English gardens are very tidy. All I wanted was to have flowers blooming in the garden from February through November."

Even so, the gardens, a mass of tall perennials, ornamental grasses, and small trees, reflect Elizabeth's eye for design, her appreciation of color and shape. "It's a challenge to design a garden so the color range will change through the seasons," she says. "I love the blues, but I've found that it's really the mixing of colors that makes each one work." Each year, the gardens' colors seem to become more bountiful and varied. Today, she says, "people stop at the gate and just stare."

The gardens begin their colorful show as the first flowers open yellow blossoms in late February. As spring progresses, pinks appear; blues come out in June and

Top: *In the back garden, the Crookhams feel hidden from the city.*

Above: *Flowers surround an 18th-century English statue in the back.*

July. White and rose tones predominate in August, and the garden finishes the season in a blaze of golds and rusts. "Not only does the color range change throughout the season, but the attitude," Elizabeth says. "Midsummer is meant to be kind of a riot. And at the end, the colors become rich and deep as fall comes on. It gets a mellow, softened look."

Behind the house, Elizabeth continued the gardens but kept the colors more subdued: Flowers bloom in muted pinks, yellows, and corals. Here the Crookhams created a secluded garden with a fenced terrace, a quiet contrast to the dazzling spectrum in front. Elizabeth calls the shadowy sanctuary her secret garden. "This is a special place, a retreat."

Stretching down the hill beyond the terrace is a third, wedge-shape garden, planted with dogwood, vine maples, and rhododendrons; bordered with azaleas, flowering clematis, and hydrangeas. In raised beds here, Elizabeth cultivates vegetables, herbs, and experimental flowers, and picks fruit from small trees.

Throughout the property, Elizabeth has given her plantings their freedom, encouraging a slightly wild, overgrown look. That gives her freedom, too—from much of the maintenance more formal gardens demand. "One of the joys of gardening," she explains, "is to have time to enjoy your creation, to relax, to sit, to visit with friends, to paint. Otherwise, what's all the effort for?" □

October

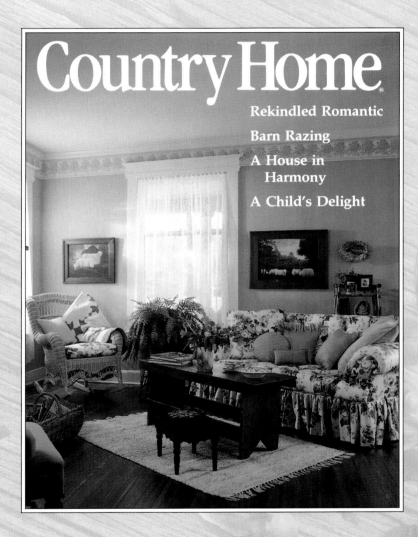

Country Home®

Rekindled Romantic

Barn Razing

A House in
Harmony

A Child's Delight

REKINDLED
Romantic

Colors had faded, the foundation was crumbling, but this turn-of-the-century Victorian home struck a responsive chord. Although the renovation project would require more than a mere dab of paint, the staff of Country Home® *magazine recognized a ready candidate for romantic revival.*

By Steve Cooper. Interior design by Joseph Boehm

Photographs by William N. Hopkins. Produced with Peggy A. Fisher. Architecture: The Design Concern. Paint, Benjamin Moore Co.; landscaping, May Seed and Nursery; settee, Ashe Corp.

Paint, Benjamin Moore; wallpaper border, Eisenhart; lace curtains, Heritage Imports; wicker rocker, Pennsylvania House; sofa, wing chair, Hickory Chair; rag rug, Pier I; sofa, pillow fabrics, Waverly; curtain rods, Kirsch; sheep paintings, Sullins House; needlepoint pillow, Katha Diddel Home Collection

REKINDLED
Romantic

Preserving a historic house is an act of faith. That was never more apparent to our *Country Home*® magazine staff than the day we decided to direct the restoration of a turn-of-the-century home in Des Moines.

It takes faith to see beyond ill-conceived designs, warped floorboards, garish wallpaper, and the effects of age. Where some might see problems, the preservationist sees possibilities. Certainly, the task was enormous. The renovated home, however, will ensure a future for a past worth saving.

Once the project was completed, the late-Victorian, shingle-style home would be garden-variety dowdy no more. The fires of romance could be rekindled.

So walk in *Country Home* magazine's paint-spattered footsteps as we apply a fresh coat of vitality and learn a new design dialect.

The home is now country, spoken in romantic tones. The formality of Victorian decor has been replaced by vibrant and seductive colors and fabrics.

Des Moines builder Jim Seaman developed the project to resell. From the beginning, he knew the house was a bargain. It was a downcast house in an upscale neighborhood; always the best of buys.

"First, location, location, location. It's in a great neighborhood. And I just fell in love with it the first time I saw it. It has a terrific lot and the house is attractive," Jim says.

It wasn't perfect, but what place is? So a few changes were planned, among them moving the front door a few feet and adding a back door and a

rear veranda.

Typically, such renovations require little more than hammers, nails, and building permits. As is increasingly common with vintage homes in fine old neighborhoods, however, the house is part of a local historic district called Owl's Head. Cities throughout the nation

Left: *The living room entices with the lush appeal of freshened late-Victorian colors and abundantly patterned Edwardian chintz.*
Top right: *An entrance foyer was created by relocating the front door. It had opened into the living room.*
Right: *Lace tied with ribbons softens dining room windows.*

Dining room: Table, Hickory Chair; valance, Eisenhart; light fixture, Thomas Industries; birdhouse, Verouden's
Foyer: Wallpaper, Gramercy; directoire benches, Hickory Chair; bench fabric, Waverly; mirror, Ballard Designs; basket, Palacek; wicker table, Pennsylvania House; lamp, Kemp & George

Curtain, pillow, and cushion fabric, Waverly; wicker furniture, Pennsylvania House; candlesticks, Ron Hardwick Collection; rug, Karastan-Bigelow; floor tiles, Summitville Tiles

have established these districts and local rehabilitation rules as a way of protecting valued architecture.

The districts keep remodelers from running amok. Someone has to guard the rich patina of gracefully aging facades against sinful uses of siding, odd windows, and backyard decking kits.

Though some cities control all changes inside and out, Des Moines's regulations cover only exteriors. Homeowners are allowed to alter interiors however they see fit.

Because governmental roadblocks can be tough to hurdle, Jim was well prepared when he appeared for the commission hearing. Like any successful applicant, he explained what changes were planned and how they would improve the house without violating its history. He illustrated his request with blueprints prepared by architectural

❧

Left: *A black Victorian rug anchors the solarium sitting area. A baby-blue tray ceiling hides air-conditioning ducts. Right: The After main-level floor plan shows how moving the front door created a logical foyer. A back door was added. Reopening an original kitchen stairway improves traffic flow. The upper floor's master bedroom area was redesigned.*

designer Marcia Lyons. The eight-member commission approved most changes with little debate.

Gaining official approval is usually a matter of bringing respect for history to a project. Meticulously crafted dwellings are a national resource worth

preserving and protecting.

Philip R. Poorman, an assistant planner for the city of Des Moines, says, "We've always realized that places like the oldest homes in Vermont and (Thomas Jefferson's) Monticello had such historic value that we

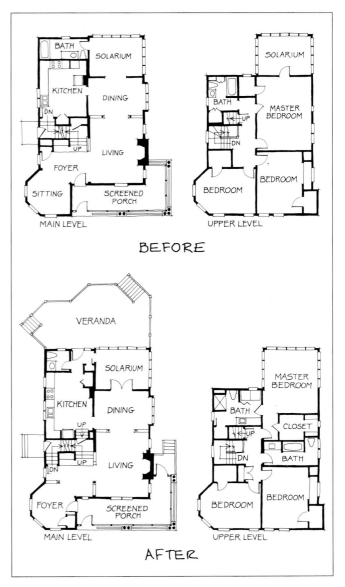

Cabinets, Plain 'n Fancy; appliances, KitchenAid; floor, Summitville Tiles; countertop, sink, Du Pont Corian;
lighting, Thomas Industries; ceilings and walls, Panora Builders

REKINDLED
Romantic

should protect them. Now we've come to realize the same is true of older colonials and Victorians."

The Rekindled Romantic house was built in 1899. As one of about 50 Owl's Head residences built through 1915, it was part of a neighborhood developed in response to the city's extension of streetcar service toward western suburbs.

Protecting such historic dwellings is only half of the problem. The more difficult step is the restoration-rebuilding process. When the hammers come out, so do the surprises.

For Jim, the wild card was a sagging foundation. One side had to be raised about a foot—not the minor repair anticipated by the developer.

Six weeks and $20,000 after the repair started, the house was level again. This was, of course, only

❧❀❧

Left: *Cabinets were chosen for both their vintage design and quality construction. A matching sink is attached to faux-marble counters. Efficient appliances make kitchen tasks a pleasure.*
Top: *Clockwise are Marcia Lyon, Steve Cooper, Joseph Boehm, and Jim Seaman.*
Right: *The wood railing of the rear veranda repeats the pattern of millwork seen around the front porch.*

preliminary to a long list of expected renovation details. Every major component of the house was rebuilt or refurbished, including heating, plumbing, electrical, floors, and walls.

Updating timeworn technologies also included repair for the home's hard-to-open, energy-wasting windows. Frames were dismantled, sash channels replaced, and cavities insulated.

Jim also did his best to flatten roller-coaster-like hard pine floors. All were sanded and refinished.

At each step, someone, whether it is a developer or a homeowner, must juggle schedules, contractors' assignments, and materials.

Jim says, "It's like

orchestrating a ballet. Early on you decide where everything goes—heating ducts, sewer lines, electrical wiring, the works—and then you move workers in and out to tackle each of their systems. But you've got to

Bed, Wesley Allen; quilt, Bartlett's; dust ruffle, Wamsutta; green, pink, and purple pillow fabrics, Waverly; pink-and-white pillows, Katha Diddel Home Collection; wallpaper border, Eisenhart; mohair throw, Mystic Valley Traders; rug, Karastan-Bigelow; chaise longue, Pennsylvania House; clock, Howard Miller

keep them from getting tangled up with each other."

What with some walls coming down and others going up, renovation jobs require the agility of an Astaire to keep everything from becoming snarled. Ironically, the purpose for all the dusty demolition was *Country Home's* determination to unsnarl rooms for improved access and circulation.

This was done downstairs by reopening a wall between the kitchen and the stairwell, by adding a back door, and by shrinking an unnecessarily large bathroom.

On the second floor, a new master suite brought a fresh vitality to what had been rooms of boxy plainness. The revamped floor layout was the answer to practical questions about bringing in groceries, getting dressed in the morning, and using otherwise fallow space.

❧◈◗❧

Left: *Master bedroom walls were painted peach, but the color was too flat. So faux finisher John Heldreth sponged on some pink.*
Top right: *The master bedroom's wallpaper border is repeated in the bathroom.*
Right: *A window seat, the focal point of the room, was given additional prominence by the placement of a fabric valance.*

As is often true with reconstruction, the project took months longer than expected. Problems that incubate for years can rarely be fixed in an hour.

Once practical issues such as heating, plumbing, and walls were settled, the fun, final shaping of interiors began.

It was like approaching a model who'd fallen on hard times. The bone structure and bearing were still there, but an undeniable weariness had taken hold. It was time to shed fading adornments dating back to the '60s and revitalize the appearances with fresh colors and textures.

Though they are soft and elegant, colors and patterns are never shy.

Rooms capture attention with lively wall paints, ivy-pattern fabrics, lacy window treatments, furniture built for lounging, plaids, and paisleys.

While Victorian homes sometimes lean a bit heavily toward the frilly

Top: Cabinet, Plain 'n Fancy; sink, shower, and fixtures, Kohler; mirror, Carolina Mirror; flooring, Armstrong World Industries; lighting, Thomas Industries; towels, JCPenney. Above: Bed and chair, Pennsylvania House; wallpaper, Eisenhart; window pillow, window seat, chair pillow, chair, and valance fabrics, Waverly; quilt, Bartlett's

141

formal, country romantic has a bit more spark. It's not a museum, but a place where people can relax and entertain. Above all, it's fun.

The romantic mood is cast upon entering the house. Sunlight sifted through lace brightens lavender walls in the living room. The room bids guests to stay.

Strong advantage is also taken of an abundance of windows at the rear of the house. Darkness isn't allowed to smother these light sources any longer. Sunshine is now showcased.

Taking care of the house was also a consideration. Who wants turn-of-the-century cleaning chores? Maintenance was considered in choosing contemporary paints,

cabinets, countertops, and other materials.

In the kitchen, handsomely crafted cabinets reflect the look of a grand era yet allow for present-day living. Dank Victorian surfaces give way to durable, fabricated faux-marble countertops and lively floor tile.

Appropriate wallpapers were important in setting the tone for the two smaller bedrooms. Feelings of softness and delicacy are enhanced by floral patterns in the young woman's room. A reflective solitude is fostered by choice of color in the gentleman's study. But paisley keeps the room from becoming too somber.

Each room is fashioned to remind us of kinder and gentler times when a peaceful color palette

included vibrant lavenders, greens, and pastels.

This was a period when rooms were elegantly costumed rather than merely decorated to serve a function.

The Rekindled Romantic is a Cinderella house proving that the dowdy can become delectable.

Romance can be rekindled, after all.

In your own backyard

If you own or are considering purchasing a house in a historic district, you need to learn about local renovation rules. Violations lead to costly repairs.

Although most historic district commissions follow federal preservation standards, these are applied in very individual ways. Most cities provide pamphlets outlining renovation policies. For further information, contact your city's planning department or historic district commission.

Information is also available in the *Directory of American Preservation Commissions*, edited by Stephen Dennis (Preservation Press, $6.95). More than 850 commissions are listed.

Editor's note: *Like a movie epic, home renovations require a huge cast. Perhaps not thousands, but certainly a large group of artists and workers.*

Among those providing their talents to the

Rekindled Romantic from the Des Moines area were:
Faux painter John Heldreth;
Woodcraft Architectural Millwork;
Panora Builders;
Servicemaster West;
Biermann University Electric Co.;
Meyers Tree Service;
Clark-Peterson Co., Inc.;
PJ Painting Plus;
Central Asphalt Paving, Inc.;
Jeff Partington Masonry;
Des Moines Marble and Mantel;
Miller English Plumbing;
Leachman Lumber Co.;
Capital Paint and Decorating;
Artistic Ornamental Iron Works;
Bankers Trust Co.;
Forman Ford Glass Co.;
Tyler Refuse, Inc.;
Ruth Barillas Wallpapering;
All State Gutters;
Overhead Door Co. of Des Moines;
Rodine Construction Co.;
Yutzy Home Improvement;
Ralph N. Smith, Inc.;
and Harold Bissell Construction.
Additional furnishings were provided by Kathy Moore, Michael Graham, and Jean Saxton.

Left: *A second-floor bedroom became a study. It's masculine attitude is beefed up with deep color, paisley-print wallpaper, and fishy accoutrements.*

Top: Carpet, Allied Fibers; rug, Pier 1; basket, Palacek. Right: Wallpaper, Eisenhart; love seat, Pennsylvania House; paint, Benjamin Moore; carpet, Allied Fibers; Oriental rug, Karastan-Bigelow; shutters, JCPenney; clock, Howard Miller; fish, W.M. Green; lamps, Frederick Cooper; ottoman fabric, F. Schumacher; love seat fabric, Waverly

Right: *The Concord, Massachusetts, home of Lynn and Barbara Wickwire looks very much like the barn* below *that once stood on their property. But the 12-foot sliding door, the sturdy fieldstone foundation, and a few short timber-frame braces are all that remain of the barn's original structure.*

$\mathcal{B}$ARN RAZING

By Steve Cooper
Produced by Jean LemMon and Joseph Boehm

When **Country Home**® *magazine was enlisted to design interiors for a* **This Old House** *television project, we thought we'd be working on a 155-year-old renovated barn. But we were in for a surprise. Close inspection revealed that the Massachusetts barn was crumbling from years of neglect. Still, the show must go on.*

Interior photographs: William Stites. Color exterior: D. Randolph Foulds. Black-and-white photographs: Richard Howard. Interior design: Joseph Boehm.

The diagnosis was as obvious as it was disheartening. The aging barn was dead as a doornail. The ravages of time, neglect, and dripping water had taken a toll.

It didn't matter that the team of attending physicians included the staff from television's *This Old House* and a national authority on timber-frame design and construction. The building couldn't be saved from terminal rot.

Fortunately, beams are replaceable. Fresh siding can be hammered on. Shoring up a foundation is possible. The patient—at least a resurrected, reconstructed version—lives again.

This story of rebirth began in Concord, Massachusetts, where Lynn and Barbara Wickwire dreamed of transforming a 155-year-old barn into a three-story home. The weathered clapboard-and-shingle structure sat adjacent to a Victorian farmhouse they purchased 13 years ago. Contemplating such a move took vision to see beyond the barn's disheveled dereliction—a past revealed in heaps of dust, cobwebs, dirt, and decomposing wood.

Despite challenging conditions, the project's potential was also apparent to producers of *This Old House*, who promised to document the renovation at the beginning of its 1989-90 season. The show's creator and executive producer, Russell Morash, again invited *Country Home* to polish the completed interior spaces, after having successfully collaborated two years ago on the Weatherbee Farm restoration. Editor Jean LemMon and interior design editor Joseph Boehm would be dispatched to Concord to create an atmosphere of warmth in the Wickwire barn's spacious rooms.

All was set until master carpenter Norm Abram and the show's new host Steve Thomas inspected

Above: *Barbara and Lynn Wickwire.*
Right: *A rag rug helps define the boundaries of the living room seating area. Large accessories and a white overstuffed sofa help fill space. "This was a no place for a lot of tiny, little things,"* Country Home® *magazine editor Jean LemMon said on the PBS television show. Older wood furniture adds a lived-in touch.*

MAIN LEVEL

SECOND LEVEL

THIRD LEVEL

𝓑ARN RAZING

Sofa, chair, Drexel Heritage; sofa table, The Lane Co.; sofa, chair fabric, F. Schumacher; pillow fabric, Gramercy; coffee table, basket, small chest, The Crate and Barrel; white lamp, George Kovacs; paint, NuBrite; lighting, Lightolier

For the occasional guest, a teal-green sleeper sofa is found in this pocket library. Country Home interior design editor Joe Boehm says, *"This small, intimate space is made more so by painting walls terra-cotta as a reflection of the floor."* This cozy room contrasts markedly to the open great-room.

$\mathcal{B}$ARN RAZING

Sleeper sofa, La-Z-Boy Chair Co.; wall paint, Pratt and Lambert; Windsor chair, Interior Resources; lamp: The Crate and Barrel; tiles, Elon; door, Morgan; door hardware, Baldwin the barn. Their studied opinion? A leaky roof and years of neglect had sapped strength from beams almost a foot thick. Hemlock and spruce were crumbling as a cancerous decay seeped through the posts and joints. Bits of wood could be chipped away with a fingernail.

Realizing the need for expert advice, Tedd Benson, an author and leading authority on the barn's timber-frame style of construction, was called to Concord from his New Hampshire workshop. After careful inspection, he agreed that the structure was beyond repair.

"It was ninety-nine percent gone. We could reuse a few pegs and a couple of braces, but very little could be saved. No one would like to have saved the original barn more than I, but you can't repair such heavy damage," Benson says.

As quickly as you could say "Plan B," a different strategy was plotted: Pull down the old barn and erect a replacement over the same foundation. The reconstructed dwelling would be similar in appearance but with interiors designed with an eye toward a different kind of creature comfort.

Though the Wickwires are jubilant with the results, the loss of the original barn was an unexpected trauma in the midst of an otherwise remarkable and positive experience for the couple. They watched as a construction crew peeled off the outer

Above: *All hands are needed to hoist beams.* Below: *Concord woodworker Bill Brace made the harvest table. Dinner conversation with guests will likely turn toward the great room's exposed beams.*

BARN RAISING

Having razed Lynn and Barbara Wickwire's barn, the *This Old House* crew launched into the chore of raising a new one.

Everyone involved agreed the new structure should be as much like the original as possible—an English-style, post-and-beam barn characterized by strength and permanence.

The show's new host, Steve Thomas, says, "It's like the old saying, 'This is my grandfather's ax. My father replaced the handle and I replaced the head.'"

Craftsman Tedd Benson directed the creation of the building's 36 × 46-foot timber frame. This is the backbone of the structure— an interlocking skeleton of rugged beams, some nearly a foot thick.

Like a choreographer gracefully moving a full stage, Benson called out the orders during what he calls "the dance of the timber framers." This was the day 90 men and (continued)

Chairs, lamp, The Crate and Barrel; windows, Marvin; plant stand, The Lane Co.; apothecary; Drexel Heritage; rug, Capel

skin of lumber and tin, attached heavy chains to the frame, and toppled the creaking beams. It was as if a museum's prized dinosaur exhibit collapsed.

"It came as a terrible blow. Living there was a part of what we had dreamed about. It was a great, great disappointment," says Barbara, a high school special-needs tutor.

There was little time for mourning, however. The project began in May 1989, and was complete five months later.

"When you're working with television, you learn to make decisions in a hurry," says Lynn, assistant director for development at Boston's Joslin Diabetes Center. "They might hand you a three-inch-thick catalog and ask for an overnight decision on all the hardware in the house. Or they might need your decision in thirty seconds. You don't mull things over."

When results were broadcast nationally in 20 episodes on PBS stations beginning last October, the grand finale featured the star—the barn-home—in full regalia. Gleaming *Country Home* interiors were dressed with fresh woods, paints, and fabrics. Spaces that had been stalls and storage in the original barn have gone upscale as people-pleasing rooms mixing the formal with the informal.

This was no small accomplishment.

"The challenge was to fill these enormous spaces. Not only that, they needed patterns, textures, and colors to bring them to life," Jean says.

The answer to never-ending space was to give definition with floor treatments. Dark rag rugs established boundaries.

women raised the barn. The day of arduous labor echoed an earlier era when neighbor helped neighbor and barn raising was a high point on a community's social calendar.

"This is serious fun. There's nothing in the world like putting a frame up," says Benson, a leader in the revival of this ancient building style.

The frame was wrapped with stress-skin panels, a multipurpose wall material made for post-and-beam construction. Because each 8-foot panel is a sandwich of exterior board, insulation, and interior finish board, several steps were saved compared with typical building. All that remained was siding outside and paint inside.

Another *(continued)*

Above: *Lowering stress-skin panels into place.* Below: *Shaker stools and painted Windsor chairs add the appeal of country to an otherwise modern kitchen.*

Appliances, Thermador-Waste King; chairs, basket, The Crate and Barrel; stools, Nichols & Stone; faucet, Friedrich Grohe; cabinets, Pioneer Craftsman; counter, backsplash tile, Latco

This family room will be a popular gathering spot with its easy access to the kitchen. The low ceiling creates intimacy, and tile flooring is warmed by a radiant-heat system. Television and electronic gear can be stored in the Scandinavian cupboard. Under the window is a decorated sleeping bench.

A pearl-gray wall paint helps set the master bedroom apart from other rooms. "This was a room for contrasts and combinations," Joe says. A rustic Scandinavian cupboard serves as counterbalance to a high-tech lamp, and a Shaker sewing table contrasts with an overstuffed sofa.

$\mathcal{B}$ARN RAZING

Bed plans, The New Yankee Workshop; wing chair, painted chest, love seat, The Crate and Barrel; pillow fabric, Gramercy; floor lamp, George Kovacs; table lamp, Stiffel; window shade, Hunter Douglas; cocktail table, Interior Resources

"When you have a big space like that it seems like the furniture is floating out in the middle of nowhere. So you create islands of intimacy in these oceans of space," Joe says.

To fill the expanse, the size of the furnishings was important. Very large sofas, chairs, and tables were ordered. Fabrics were light to seemingly increase the furniture's size.

"And we brought in some wonderful old pieces—the great rugged coffee table, for example. These things give a room a sense of having been lived in. A sense of life. They take the cold, sterile look out of a contemporary room," Jean says.

When all was complete, the barn was a success for *Country Home, This Old House,* and, most of all, for the Wickwires. It re-created the timber-frame beauty of the original structure yet gave the couple a comfortable home for modern living.

In the process, the Wickwires were also changed. Their television appearance bestowed a status of instant celebrity on them.

Lynn says, "It's kind of a funny thing becoming a celebrity, even if just for a few weeks. It was like people were living their dreams vicariously through us.

"Just last week we were in Times Square in New York when this man came up and stopped us. 'Aren't you the Wickwires?' he asked, and proceeded to say how he loved the show. Amazing." □

Below: *A faux-grained chest and a hooked rug add charm to the third-floor bedroom. Drapery treatment heightens awareness of the room's location as it echoes the peak of the ceiling. Because the Wickwires' children are grown, only a daybed is needed.*

unusual aspect of the house is its in-floor radiant heating system. Water heated in the basement is pumped through pipes snaked under the floor. As the floor tiles warm up, spaces are heated evenly and silently.

Learning to use the system did take some practice because of a lag between turning the system on and getting heat. Once they adapted, however, the Wickwires were sold.

After living with the house for a few months, the Wickwires say their barn home is near perfect.

"At times, I didn't see how we would get finished," Barbara says. "But everyone, including *Country Home,* pitched in and pulled together."

Proving that even when hopes are razed, hard work will raise them again. □

Daybed, Wesley Allen; carpet, Du Pont Stainmaster, Gulistan Stevens; fabrics, F. Schumacher & Co.; round cricket table, Lane; lamp, Tyndale/Frederick Cooper; chair, botanical prints, The Crate and Barrel

· A House in ·
HARMONY

By Molly Culbertson
Produced with Ann Omvig Manternach

On a tree-shaded hilltop, in their house built from Tennessee's past, Radney and Mary-Springs Foster find a quiet retreat from nearby Nashville and Radney's singing career.

♦ ♦ ♦

Opposite: *The beginnings of the Fosters' house were found in a late 18th-century house located in middle Tennessee. That one-room structure is now the Fosters' living room.*

"We wanted a simple place that we could grow with, that would be a reflection of us," says Radney Foster, a young country musician in Nashville. He and his wife, Mary-Springs, knew they wanted an older home.

"Radney and I both are connected with families that belonged to older homes," Mary-Springs says. "We wanted to be connected with the past that way, too." He grew up in west Texas, she in the Carolinas.

The Fosters moved to Tennessee so that Radney could establish himself as a singer and guitarist. They were drawn to the country for its quiet refuge from the hectic life-style that has accompanied Radney's career. This desire for sanctuary and their passion for the past led them to build a home south of Nashville. The two-part harmony of the structure—part old, part new—is said by some experts to be one of the best restoration and reconstruction projects in recent Tennessee history.

The effort poured into the design and construction of the house is evident today in every detail. The place has the presence of a venerable building that has been lived in and loved for many generations. As they worked on the restoration, they tried to understand what the original inhabitants wanted, to create a house that they would have liked, explains longtime friend Robert

Left: *Architects used 19th-century plans to create the two-story addition and wraparound porch.*
Above: *Radney and Mary-Springs Foster enjoy the quiet that surrounds their home in the Tennessee countryside.*

♦ ♦ ♦

· A House in ·
HARMONY

• • •

Crafting Caledonia: Re-creating Early Tennessee Artistry

From the beginning, Mary-Springs and Radney Foster and architectural historian Robert Hicks agreed to search out local craftspeople to work on the Fosters' house. Shown on these pages are just a few examples of the work the team executed for the project.

Local blacksmith Doyle

• • •

Opposite: The large, open kitchen and dining room are in the two-story addition. The Fosters are furnishing their home gradually, searching for pieces made in southern

Hicks, an expert on southern antiques and historic architecture who is avid about saving the pre-Civil War houses still standing in Tennessee.

Mary-Springs agrees that the house does, indeed, have the spirit of a well-aged place. "We talk sometimes about whether the ghosts from the old house came with us when we tore it down and moved it here," she says, laughing. "We're delighted."

Before the Fosters moved in, they christened the house Caledonia after a plantation near Charleston that was the summer home of Mary-Springs' family. "We all felt that the house had grown enough by the time we were finished that it needed a name," Robert says. Caledonia, as Scotland was once called, seemed an especially appropriate name for a place built by Scottish settlers.

Inspiration for the design of their home came from Robert. While traveling the back roads of Williamson County around Nashville, he discovered a two-room house built in 1792. Though there seemed barely enough of the house left to keep it upright, Robert and other architectural historians in the area investigated the remains of the ramshackle structure. They decided that this truly was a worthy example of 18th-century architecture.

Its construction is typical of many Scotch-Irish houses built before the Civil War in the backcountry of Tennessee, the Carolinas, and Virginia, Robert explains. "We like to think of our southern history in terms of grand old houses." But before the mansions there were modest, vernacular houses built by settlers. "Some of them were fine and full of grace," he says. Many of them have been lost to age, neglect, and a preference for more modern dwellings.

"When I found out that the land had been sold out from underneath the house, and the house was going to have to go, I took Radney and Mary-Springs out to see it," Robert says.

Something about it appealed to them, too. Mary-Springs says, "Helping to tear it down and move it here, piece by piece, made us feel strongly about it."

From that small, aged dwelling, Robert conceived a design for the Fosters' home. The goal was to preserve the integrity of the original 1792 structure and also provide the Fosters with a comfortable home. He decided that the house, once completed, would appear to have been built over a 100-year period, with the new win-

Neeley used Early American techniques to create locks and strap hinges (shown *above*) for the doors.

And when it came time for lighting fixtures, including the dining room chandelier shown *opposite* and the wall sconces *above*, the Fosters called on friend and tinsmith Charles Baker, who drove to Tennessee from his home in North Carolina for frequent visits throughout the   *(continued)*

• • •

Tennessee during the early 1800s. "We're going slowly, looking for things that are appropriate for the house and buying them as we can afford them," says Mary-Springs.

155

·A House in·
HARMONY
• • •

gan accurate reproduction of a 19th-century country house.

Radney and Mary-Springs agreed with Hicks that patterns tied historically to the area should be used throughout the house, and when possible, they should hire local crafts-people to do the work. The Fosters, Hicks, and contractor Sandy Lawton assembled a project team that included finish carpenters, cabinetry specialists, a blacksmith, an authority on historic colors, a tinsmith, and others. "We were incredibly fortunate to work with so many talented folks," Robert says. He credits architect Jim Pomy for giving life to the original concept.

When reassembly of the 1792 house began, the team discovered that so little of the original structure existed that they needed additional research help to put it all together. For direction, Robert sought the help of friends he had made through his research and study of southern material culture. Among the experts on southern antiquities who came to Nashville to consult on the project were John Bivins from North Carolina (a past director of restoration at Old Salem), and Wendell Garrett from New York, editor of *Antiques* magazine.

As many 19th-century pieces as could be found were put into the new house. Robert discovered the 1820s stairway in pieces in a Nashville subdivision, floorboards in another tumbledown dwelling, and fragments of wood trim in yet another. Those pieces of the past were duplicated by hand to create an illusion of age. Once the basic construction and craftwork were finished, "we let the house evolve as it would have throughout the 1800s," Robert says. "We added a porch on the two-story section, then filled it in so that it wraps around the house."

The upstairs—two bedrooms, guest room, and bath—is still unfinished, and will remain so until the couple can afford to complete the rooms with the same care given the rest of the house.

Today, the Fosters' Caledonia is a tribute to early Tennessee architecture. "We hope our house is an inspiration to other people who are interested in restoration," Mary-Springs says.

"We love the place," adds Radney. "I'm out on the road on tour so much—a very different environment. It's wonderful to come home and get in touch with what's real."

(continued) construction of Caledonia.

When Hicks found the staircase, disassembled in the basement of a house in a Nashville subdivision, only a short segment of the original hand-carved woodwork was still intact. Local craftspeople re-created it and duplicated the slight imperfections in the curves.

The team of artists and craftspeople who worked on the house assembles on Caledonia's front porch. Bottom row, from left: Jim Pomy, architect; Mary-Springs and basset Beau; Hicks; William Knight,

• • •

Opposite: *The master bedroom, overlooking a wooded ravine, is in the new wing of the house. The doors at the right open onto a small back porch.*

In May this year, Mary-Springs began working on a

electrician; Virginia Hunter, the paint specialist who helped create historically accurate colors for interior and exterior walls and trim; and Charles Baker, tinsmith. Second row, from left: Radney; Vernon Morris, cabinetmaker; Doyle Neeley, blacksmith; Sidney (Suds) Quarrier, one of the carpenters; Alan Duke, who supplied many new materials for the house; and Richard Warrick, who supplied old material for the house. □

• • •

historic garden behind the house. She worked with local horticulturists to find flowers and herbs that would have been in a kitchen garden in the 18th and 19th centuries.

In 1833, a horticulturist wrote an inspirational children's book on gardening. Today, his legacy flourishes in a small garden re-created especially for the joys of young visitors at Old Sturbridge Village.

A Child's DELIGHT

By Molly Culbertson
Produced by Estelle Bond Guralnick

Above: *Throughout the summer, children of employees at the village don their own 19th-century costumes and help tend the gardens. Here, one young, but enthusiastic, gardener examines coreopsis.*

Right: *The entire Fitch Garden is only 15 feet in diameter. Horticulturist Joseph Breck designed the center arbor as a walk-through in 1833, but in Old Sturbridge Village, full undergrowth prevents access and protects delicate plants.*

Opposite: *Vining sweet peas completely camouflage the birch saplings that are woven together to form the central arbor. Between the garden and the Fitch house's barn, an Old Sturbridge Village employee hangs laundry to dry.*

In the living museum of Old Sturbridge Village in Massachusetts, children can frolic among the flowers—just as 19th-century horticulturist Joseph Breck intended.

Through his book, *The Young Florist; or Conversations on The Culture of Flowers, and on Natural History,* Breck extolled the virtues of tending a garden. Such activity, he believed, taught children not only flora and fauna, but also the fine rewards reaped by industrious recreation.

It was Breck's work that garden historian Christie White interpreted to create the children's garden at Sturbridge Village. Called the Fitch Garden, the space is small—only 15 feet by 15 feet. Yet its bounty includes nearly 25 varieties of flowering

plants, each selected to fascinate children with its powerful fragrance, bright blossom, unusual texture, or other curiosity.

In *The Young Florist,* Breck—with the help of his two young characters, siblings Henry and Margaret—takes us

through a gardener's year. Breck used the twosome's childish dialogues to show how to create continuous color from April through the first frost in the fall. He offered information about a variety of perennials, biennials, and annuals—their history

Had we a perpetual summer and a continued succession of flowers, we should perhaps soon become indifferent, and esteem them of little value.

—Joseph Breck, *The Young Florist*

Opposite: *The garden stands only a few feet from the Fitch House. In the 1800s, when decorative gardening first began to fill Americans' leisure time, gardeners always laid out their plots within full view of a window.*

Above top: *Bachelor's buttons are sometimes called cornflowers. That name comes from England, where the flower was considered a nuisance to farmers—blossoms often would appear, unwanted, in fields of grain.*

Above bottom: *Balsam is an old-fashioned flower sometimes called lady's slipper, named for the shape of its delicate flower.*

A Child's
DELIGHT

introduction into American home gardens, and their proper care and cultivation.

Today, Sturbridge Village horticulturists pass along Breck's colorful legacy to young visitors, who require little encouragement to wander into the Fitch Garden. "The layout itself is inviting," Christie says of the circular path between the central arbor and the outer border. "There's something elemental about circles—and children seem to pick up on that." The garden's simplicity also lends appeal, Christie says. "Children can imagine going home and building their own arbor from sticks like the birch-sapling

arbor here, and collecting their own wild plants."

All plants in the garden are intended to keep a child's attention. Plants are chosen by category—there are scented, old-fashioned, exotic, wild, and curious plants. The last category includes the sensitive plant, whose leaves curl when touched. "I've watched three-year-olds kneel in front of a sensitive plant for twenty minutes, stroking each leaf until it closes," Christie says. Nearby, the unicorn plant attracts children with its brown, clawlike seedpod.

Other, more familiar flowering plants grow here, too. Many bloom at different times of day, so

GARDEN KEY

The illustration above shows the general layout of the Fitch Garden. The plants here include:

1. *Four o'clock*
2. *Ox-eye daisy*
3. *Scarlet runner bean*
4. *Balsam*
5. *Morning-glory*
6. *Sweet pea*
7. *Maltese cross*
8. *Foxglove*
9. *Calendula*
10. *Violet*
11. *Coreopsis*
12. *Alyssum*
13. *Bluebottle*
14. *Mignonette*
15. *Sweet William*
16. *Catchfly*
17. *Heartsease*
18. *Wild geranium*
19. *Clarkea*
20. *Bluebottle*
21. *Sensitive plant*
22. *Evening primrose*
23. *Coltsfoot*
24. *Martynia*

Right top: *Coreopsis is an annual native to Arkansas. In the 1800s, a botanist gathered its seeds and took them east.*

Right bottom: *This sweet allysum is an older variety than the one that grows in many home gardens today. It also is known as clarkea— Lewis and Clark were responsible for transporting it from the west to the east. It is related to the pansy.*

Above: *This is balloon vine, also known as love-in-a-puff. Each seed inside the tiny green pods is marked with a perfect white heart.*

*T*he garden continued its gorgeous appearance until the last of the month, when there came a frost sufficiently heavy to destroy the tender annuals.

—Joseph Breck on an autumn garden, *The Young Florist*

there is color all day long. Morning-glories open their blooms early, then fade just as the four o'clocks begin to flower.

Vining sweet peas and scarlet runner beans grow on the central arbor; underneath are tulips, daffodils, and narcissus that bloom in early spring. Later, monkshood, balsams, and scarlet lychnis fill their space.

Fragrant plants, like mignonette and four o'clocks, are planted to attract dragonflies, butterflies, and moths. The flying insects, Breck wrote, provide more intrigues for neophyte gardeners.

When Breck published his book more than 150 years ago, decorative gardening was a new and popular recreation in this country. It began, ironically, with the machine age, which provided Americans with more free time than they'd ever known. At the same time, advancements in printing made it possible to publish volumes of garden manuals and seed catalogs—which made gardening seem irresistible.

Early American gardeners favored the romantic gardens of England. They built arbors and trellises to support vining, lacy plants that provided a lush background for vivid blooms. Their gardens included more variety, more brilliant color, and more potent aromas than

today's gardens.

Hybridization has reduced the intensity of color and fragrance in many garden flowers. So Christie has used the old-fashioned and wild plants to entice Fitch Garden visitors. The result is that Breck's theory is proved each day, as children spend many quiet moments examining the plant life.

With her work in the garden, Christie shares with others a belief that Breck also held—

ornamental gardening is among the healthiest, most enjoyable, and most educational of children's leisure pursuits. □

Editor's note: *Old Sturbridge Village re-creates an 1830s New England town. Here, people in historical dress demonstrate early 19th-century life, work, and celebrations. For information, write to OSV, 1 Old Sturbridge Village Rd., Sturbridge, MA 01566-1198; phone 508/347-3362.*

A Child's DELIGHT

December

Country Home®

All in a Name
White Christmas
One from the Hearth

All in a Name

Christmas Tree Farm isn't a place for the commercial cutting of spruces or balsam firs. A rustic Maine farmhouse so named for its special holiday charm, it is the year-round home of wood-carver Huston Clark Sieburth and family.

By Candace Ord Manroe
Produced by Estelle Bond Guralnick

Left: *The keeping room showcases an early-1800s New England settle; late-1700s stool; the chair table bought from the home's former owner; an early-1800s Nova Scotian dresser,* right, *and Clark's carvings,* top. Below: *Wood carver Clark Sieburth with wife Carole and son Nathan.*

In Nova Scotia, the Bay of Fundy is renowned for having the world's highest tide. In the harbor town of Cutler, Maine, the mouth of Fundy opens to create what locals declare to be the world's thickest and fastest-appearing fog. When the fog rolls in, temperatures can drop 20 degrees in a matter of minutes.

Clark and Carole Sieburth didn't know any of that in 1984, when they were looking to escape a different kind of density—too many people—in the midcoast region of the state.

Almost halfway to the North Pole and sparsely populated, Cutler offered ample elbowroom and unspoiled beauty. It also presented the ideal home: an antique Cape on picturesque grounds. And as an 11th-generation New Englander and a native of Maine, Carole didn't object to planting roots in her home state.

Clark and Carole visited the circa-1820 house in August.

"It was hot, but all I could visualize was how the house would look with Christmas wreaths on all three doors and candles in the windows. We love Christmas—a traditional holiday celebration," says Clark.

All in a Name

Left: *Original finishes decorate the keeping room's preserve cupboard and circa-1800 chair table.*
Opposite: *Clark's Père Nöel carving is at home on a scroll-leg, circa-1770 bench in the parlor. The table is early 18th century.*
Above: *Clark's Santas fill the 1820 home below.*

Clark hadn't begun carving Santas and Father Christmases when the couple bought the home and named it Christmas Tree Farm. The Sieburths' intense regard for the holiday, coupled with the property's profuse firs and spruces, was reason enough for the name.

"Our season starts around Thanksgiving, when the fruitcakes are baked and decorating begins," says Carole. "Even though Clark is busy with carvings almost up until Christmas, we bake seven hundred to eight hundred Christmas cookies to deliver to friends and neighbors."

Other holiday traditions include the New England custom of oyster stew for Christmas Eve dinner, and Cornish hens on Christmas Day. Dried rosehips and herbs grown on the farm are part of decorating, along with holly, flowers, fruits, and

nuts—"simple things that make us and our friends feel peaceful, happy, and relaxed," says Carole.

The entire family, including son Nathan, enjoy researching Christmas traditions from around the world, then incorporating favorite customs into their own celebration.

168

Left: *Kitchen storage consists of a late-1700s Maine cupboard in original red paint, with Clark's belsnickel on the step.*
Right: *Painted thumb-back 1830s Windsor chairs flank the kitchen's Sheraton-style table.*
Below: *The dining room is festive with Clark's art, top.*

All in a
Name

Fragrances of frankincense and myrrh fill the home, along with the crisper scents of fresh balsam fir and spruce. Each holiday the family cuts at least three spruce trees from the property, then decorates each one in a different style.

The keeping room tree is laden with decorations handmade from natural materials—"cornhusks, wheat weavings, beeswax, and small carved wood birds," says Carole. "This is our country tree, as opposed to the parlor's more formal tree."

Given the family's regard for Christmas, it isn't surprising that, their first season in the home, Carole requested a Father Christmas as her gift. Clark had been carving as a hobby since age 5, when he received his first whittling tools from his father. He had never carved a human figure, though, and decided it was time. Soon, the name of the Sieburth home serendipitously had acquired yet another meaning: Clark returned to Christmas subjects again and again in his carving.

By the spring of 1985, carving—or, as some see it, wood sculpting—had become his full-time vocation.

171

All in a Name

Opposite: *The bedroom's circa-1690 Carver chair is draped by a crib quilt. An 1821 pegged blanket chest topped by Clark's farmer carving boasts original red paint. Left: A late-1600s candle holder warms the late-1700s country Hepplewhite table. Top: Clark's art.*

Formerly a professional magician, cook, and baker, Clark had worked out of his fields after moving to Cutler. His career as carver was launched on a $20 nest egg.

Today Clark's work, which specializes in Santas and Father Christmases, is considered by his collectors to be the finest in the medium.

"I am self-taught," he says, "both in carving and painting. I work in native white pine using only hand tools, and my work is known both for my fine detail and original designs," he adds.

As a Mainer, Clark is carrying on a time-honored tradition. The state has a rich heritage of wood-carvers and is known as the Pine Tree State. "But I am not trying to re-create a legacy, as in reproduction work. I am attempting to create a new one," Clark insists.

He takes no shortcuts along the way: "I use hand tools because I feel that the quality of the work I produce can be created by no other methods. I still do all of the carving and painting myself and will continue to do so," he says.

The family's interest in international Christmas traditions provides a rich repository of ideas for Clark's subjects. "My Father Christmases and Santas are inspired by many different ethnic and regional traditions," he says.

And according to Carole, "many people of European descent identify figures of Clark's and are quite excited by them. His various Father Christmases strike a deep responsive note with people who view them," she says.

Clark, Carole, and Nathan transform their separation from the

All in a Name

Right: *Clark carves at his worktable in a corner of the keeping room.*
Left: *His outpouring includes not only Christmas figures but patriotic chickens, roosters, pumpkins, and fish.*
Below: *This home's heart belongs to Christmas.*

mainstream into an opportunity to pursue favorite interests. All three are fascinated with New England history and antiques, and, with no TV to distract them, spend cold nights perusing their more than 3,000 books. They've especially enjoyed exploring the history of their own home, which was built by Samuel Holmes Davis.

A Davis descendant, 98-year-old Minerva Ackley, visited the Sieburths and shared invaluable information, even as to where the Davises used to position their Christmas tree: "The same place we put ours," Clark says.

With this personal link to their home's history, the Sieburths have an especially warm environment for displaying lovingly collected antiques—Carole's early woodenware and pre-1830 New England redware, and Clark's early glass and ceramics. "Mostly, we try to collect things that have a feel or aura to them, some intangible sense of the past owners," Clark says.

At Christmas, past and present become one in the Sieburths' celebration of tradition. "It's our time to reflect on another year gone by, to really sit still and appreciate what we have," Clark says. □

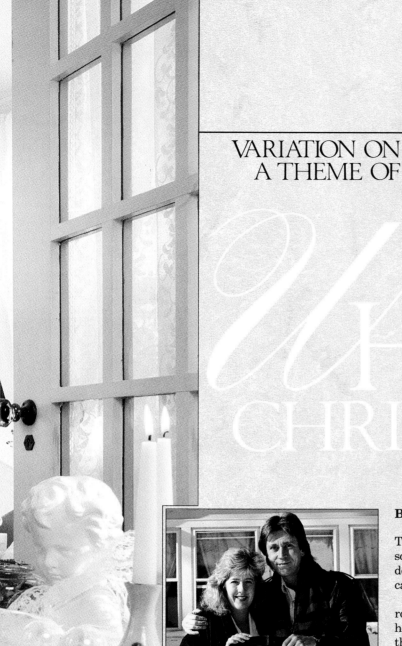

VARIATION ON A THEME OF

White Christmas

Jennifer and Jeff Buya make sure Christmas in their Chicago-suburb cottage is white— with or without snow.

By Candace Ord Manroe

The color of romance isn't valentine blush or sophisticated black, but white—a fact well documented by Jennifer and Jeff Buya's Chicago-area cottage home.

By self-admission, the newlyweds are both romantics. Unlike the hackneyed phrase, however, there's nothing *helpless* about them. Jennifer and Jeff don't rely on blind luck to bring them a white Christmas—the romantic backdrop they hold imperative for this holiday season of *true* love, warm hearts, and giving.

Should the snow happen to be on the ground, fine. Hot drinks and a blazing fire are all they must add. But should Christmas Day be dry, with nary a snowflake in sight, that's OK, too. The Buyas hold an insurance policy: an interior that's holiday-adorned in a blanket of soft white textiles trimmed with shimmering silver ornaments and accessories, down to the ribbons and wrappings.

As owner of Amazing Lace, Jennifer has no dearth of old and new lacework on hand.

Left: Ornaments from both Jennifer's childhood and her lace shop decorate the live Scotch pine in the sun-room of the couple's 75-year-old Chicago-area cottage, top.

WHITE
CHRISTMAS

Throughout the year, the couple's 75-year-old cottage in the Chicago suburbs a quarter mile from Lake Michigan wears a lacy mantle. Virtually nothing escapes a filigreed drape—not windows, tabletops, pillows, or even the living room sofa, which is covered with filet lace from the 1920s.

"The living room is our escape room," says Jennifer. "Even when it's not Christmas, I like to throw different lace tablecloths over the sofa in there."

Christmas, though, is the time when the year-round lace is augmented by strictly seasonal romantic indulgences. Wispy angel hair appears in unlikely places: entwined between a pair of small Staffordshire dogs, generously strewn over cut boughs in a wicker planter, and even mounted atop the headboard of the guest room's antique bed.

Top: *A favorite antique birdcage shares the mantel with stockings made by a friend.*
Right: *Antique lace from the couple's honeymoon in England covers the living room's tea table.*

WHITE CHRISTMAS

Baby's-breath and white tulips fill country containers. Opalescent tree ornaments not only decorate the living room's towering Scotch pine but appear in less expected places as simple design elements in holiday vignettes created on tabletops.

And to this white Christmas, Jennifer's collection of antique birdcages and her live white doves add their own share of magic.

"Originally I started buying cages to use as window treatments," says Jennifer. "A friend gave me a pair of doves, and I soon had a fast-growing collection of both doves and cages."

Synonymous with peace, the white doves imbue the holiday's quiet times with a special serenity. One such time was a candlelight champagne breakfast Christmas morning. It was then that Jeff presented Jennifer with appropriate gifts—an antique English sterling silver lovebirds brooch, and a black velvet robe trimmed in Battenberg lace.

But Jeff hasn't always been such a savvy romantic. "Until I met Jennifer, I'd never given flowers to anyone but my mother. My

Opposite: *Vintage 1910 crocheted lace on the table says white Christmas in the dining room.*
Left: *Doves, dogs, and lace create a vignette.*
Top: *The '30s stove works—and cost $35.*

181

WHITE CHRISTMAS

condo wasn't furnished in lace, yet I enjoy what she's done here. I guess Jennifer has brought out the romantic in me," he says.

What Jennifer refers to as her "Joan Crawford room" is proof of her own ability as romantic dramatist. With its fringed lamp and floral walls, the upstairs retreat exudes a flamboyance reminiscent of '40s films. Pearl beads and lace spill out of floral hatboxes amid piles of presents. A collection of antique Staffordshire figures clustered atop Victorian antiques adds to the vintage flair.

"I believe it's important to surround yourself with the things that you love, to create an environment that's comfortable and inviting. You don't have to spend a fortune. I've been buying antiques since I was seventeen, and for the first ten years I collected, I rarely spent more than two hundred dollars for any furnishing," she says.

It isn't too surprising to learn of that economy. Money not only can't buy love, it apparently can't buy a white Christmas, either. Like romance, that takes heart. □

Top: *The "Joan Crawford room" exemplifies Jennifer's flair for the romantic and dramatic.*
Right: *With bears taking tea, a guest room is ready for visits from Jeff's young daughter.*

One from the
HEARTH

Despite living near San Diego, Barbara Strickland longed for a New England country house. Now she and her husband have it without leaving the West Coast.

Above: *Behind Bert and Barbara Strickland is a portrait of their granddaughter, Veronica, that was painted by Barbara.*

Below right: *It's another green Christmas at the Stricklands'.*

Opposite: *Barbara painted the checkerboard, the portrait above the mantel, and the gourd Santas. She finished the pine paneling with linseed oil and made the wreaths.*

By Steve Cooper

The houses on Bert and Barbara Strickland's street are not much different than those found in other middle-class Southern California neighborhoods. These low-slung, ranch-style designs are as pervasive as sunshine.

From a distance, the Stricklands' home doesn't appear to stray far from the pattern. A closer look, however, reveals a dash of individuality: Board-and-batten replaces the standard stucco exterior; instead of a typical bay, there are multipane windows. These touches merely hint at the home's departure from suburban design lockstep. Even more convincing evidence is inside the entry.

Crossing the threshold is a step back into country-style colonial. A wall of stained raised panels and a red brick hearth transport the living room back in time. A mood of refined craftsmanship is maintained with a settle finished in a rich tawny stain, an expansive flat-weave rug, and artwork in 18th-century styles.

"I've tried to create the sense of being in New England. I don't know why I love the look, but I always have. There's just something magnetic about it to me," says Barbara, a native Californian.

Enamored by eastern ways, she has brought them into her seasonal celebrations. Last year, she created a "Colonial Williamsburg Christmas" for her family. This year, she plans a "Massachusetts Christmas."

"Most of the family

184

Photographs: William N. Hopkins, Hopkins Associates.

hasn't been to visit Williamsburg. So this was a way to take them there. I bought a Williamsburg cookbook, played my tape of Williamsburg music, and wore my long dress with a homespun apron. It was a big hit with the grandchildren," she says.

Freshly prepared ham, peanut soup, and pecan pie graced the table. Among the dozen family members in attendance was Barbara's mother, 85-year-old Susie Angle, and she enthusiastically approved.

"She used to think my love for the East was a bit crazy. But I've even won my mother over, and now the family has a new Christmas tradition. We'll go somewhere new each year—right here in the living room," Barbara says.

Long before she first visited the East Coast in 1976, Barbara was entranced by the colonial ambience. Barbara's infatuation began in a childhood friend's San Diego home.

The friend's mother had a particularly deft decorating touch, which she employed by creating a graceful haven filled with comfortable Americana. It didn't matter that red tile roofs and an adobe look dominate San Diego.

"The use of older furniture with an eastern flavor sparked something in me that's remained. I'm glad she had enough confidence in her own taste to buck the local trends," Barbara says.

Not that the Stricklands' interiors sprang forth fully developed. Rooms evolved during the 35 years the couple have owned their coastal abode.

The living room was paneled 23 years ago. The Stricklands began

One from the
HEARTH

Left: *The dining room chairs are reproductions made from kits. Barbara chose her subject on the wall to reflect the austerity of Early American portraiture. "I love the dark, pious looks," she says.*

Above: *The combined colors and textures of Virginia creeper and Mexican peppers work well together in a tree Barbara fashioned. Though they look like wood, the eggs in the basket are the real thing. Patterns were scratched into goose eggs after they were boiled with onion.*

purchasing reproduction furniture kits 15 years ago. A decade ago the original bay window was replaced. Barbara began adding her artwork in 1983.

"It didn't happen overnight. We kind of progressed to where we are as money and time allowed," she says.

Bert was happy to play second fiddle as Barbara orchestrated changes. He saved his artistry for his career as a barber.

"She was the one with the eye for all this and the enthusiasm. Frankly, it took me years before I loved it too," Bert says.

He began his own discoveries during their first trip East. Now, both look forward to their frequent treks around museums, inns, and woods of the Colonies.

They spend a good deal of their time foraging for rose hips, boxwood, and wild grasses that become wreaths and arrangements not generally found in the San Diego area.

"I suppose we'd move there if we didn't have so many connections here in Southern California. But both of our sons, our grandchildren, other family, and our friends are here. That makes a place your home, doesn't it?" Barbara asks.

Since they can't uproot themselves, they are doing the next best thing: They share their love of the East by taking along grandchildren.

For several years, these forays were funded with carefully saved pennies. But when Barbara took up painting, her artwork began supplying the necessary legal tender.

"This has really enriched our lives. For most of my life I never

One from the HEARTH

Left: *The Stricklands transformed an ordinary bedroom into a sitting room by adding a pine floor, converting a closet into an alcove, and filling it with a spinning wheel, a reproduction cupboard, and Barbara's paintings.*

Above: *A collection of Barbara's artwork, including a Santa dummy board, a painting, game boards, dry herb arrangements, and a bandbox. She says, "A lot of people could do all this, if they were willing to try. But too many just assume they can't. Pick up a brush and try it."*

One from the
HEARTH

thought I'd even get back there. Now, we're able to go again and again. It's my dream come true," Barbara says.

Her art career started without many preliminaries when she picked up a brush in the early 1980s.

"No classes. Folk art painters taught themselves, so I thought I should, too," she says.

Barbara mimicked those styles she gravitated to while browsing in museums. Among these were colonial-era silent companions, also called dummy boards.

These almost life-size silhouettes were realistically painted and propped in windows. A simple security device, these silent companions could trick snooping scalawags into believing homes were occupied.

"Now, they're conversation pieces. They set my work apart because so few artists make them," she says.

Barbara sells her work through shops and also during invitational gatherings twice a year in her home. Hundreds attend to purchase artwork and New England greenery, flowers, and herbs. Bird carver and furnituremaker Ernie Williams and toy maker Ann Bruce also display work during the shows.

"We've found a strong desire for bits of New England here in our area," Barbara says.

She enjoys encouraging others who are also attempting to break with the fashion status quo. All it takes is a good eye and endless hours of work.

Barbara laughs and says, "It's amazing what you can do in thirty-five years." □

Above: *One of Barbara's favorite pieces is this sitting-room bench. The pattern for the silent companion painting was an actor she saw while visiting Old Sturbridge Village two years ago. "I like to fill my house for the Christmas season. Of course, I want it to look like Christmas in 1800," she says. Room design needn't be dictated by finances. "Young women seem to think that they can't afford the styles they love. Nonsense. I hand them a catalog and tell them to start building their own," she says.*

Index